Standing in the Chaos

Poems

Standing in the Chaos
Poems

Howard F. Stein

International Psychoanalytic Books (IPBooks)
New York • http://www.IPBooks.net

Standing in the Chaos–Poems

Published by IPBooks, Queens, NY

Online at: www.IPBooks.net

ISBN: 978-1-956864-66-3

I dedicate this book to Peter Petschauer,
Whose Abiding Friendship Fills Oceans

Contents

CONTENTS

Foreword

Standing in the Chaos is a book of wise, humane and deeply-felt poems. Howard F. Stein doesn't shy away from what, in another era, might be called political, but in our world today are really existential.

Stylistically direct, some might even be called prose/poems, but all are informed by his deep faith.

We learn from his Introduction that he understands his own poems better than even the best reader, but you will be the judge of that.

Irene Willis, Poetry Editor, IPBooks

Introduction

Standing in the Chaos brings together both published and unpublished poems on the lived experience of chaos, somehow standing, maintaining a foothold, observing in its midst, feeling all the torrential emotions it evokes, bearing witness to its reality, and not being pulled under in its violent undertow. It is about what it is and has been like to live in the United States from the early 1980's through the present – roughly from the Age of Ronald Reagan through the yet-uncompleted Age of Donald Trump, and the merciless invasion of Ukraine by Russia in February 2022.

The poems describe and evoke its noxious atmosphere. They attempt to make sense of that life, learn from it, and help readers (and beyond) to gain access to the maelstroms that come from simply dwelling during these times – and come to take up residence in the inner world as well. The poems portray my own struggle to maintain a foothold amid the violent currents that would drown me in them. *Standing in the Chaos* consists of 103 poems, some short, others long.

The question always arises about any poetry book: What is this book *about*? For poetry and all art, there cannot be a simple, direct, linear answer. As composer Gustav Mahler is reputed to have replied when asked why he wrote music: "If I could say it in words, then I would not have to write music." So, I defer the answer(s), over time, to you, my reader and companion. I will try to say here only a little about where I sense the poems in this book, and the book itself, come from.

To say that in large part they emerge from my learning to trust and follow my unconscious promptings is the beginning, not the end, of my making sense of the story of their creation. Poetry for me is an intimate conversation between myself (myselves) and the world. Seventy-eight years have taught me that I navigate an unsteady ship in a world that offers too many answers, tolerates too few questions, and leaves little creative, "potential space" (D.W. Winnicott) for gentle silence in which thoughts might be born.

Psychoanalysis has long attended to the inner, unconscious life, and how it percolates through the human body, thinking, feeling, and acting (often en-acting out-of-awareness dramas). Over more recent decades, many psychoanalysts have come to explore the never-ending dance between life in the outer world and its reverberations in and with the unconscious, and then back out again. Reality and representation are symbiotic partners in eternal – often deadly – dialogue. This is the sense-of-place and space from which my poems emerge.

If, as their *writer*, they are "mine," they are never entirely private property. They are simultaneously "yours" and "mine": that is, "ours." As I write poetry, I often feel like a *scribe*. I have come to trust – though not always – where the dance and the

2

dancing will take me. When I arrive (at a completed poem), I at once recognize it and have no idea how I got there. I could never have consciously planned the path I could only have discovered at the end of the journey. I am left in wonder: did I write the poem, or did the poem write me? I stay with the question.

Even the book's title is not altogether my own! The title of this book emerged from my long-time friend and co-author Seth Allcorn's and my recurrent use of an image and metaphor: we are standing in a swift, dangerous stream, feet slightly spread apart and firmly planted, letting the water rush between and around our legs. In the process we avoid being pulled under (by anxiety) and drowning but maintain our foothold and *observe* (as in "observing ego") the process. My guess is that Seth used this "methodological" image first, but as with all that we do, whatever originated long ago as his idea or mine, quickly becomes part of our unconscious and conscious associations, that is, it soon becomes *ours*. ("inter-subjective"). Neither of us needs to know whose original "intellectual property" it was.

Poet John Keats wrote that one of the highest virtues in life is to create a lot of mental space for "not knowing," for not *having* to know, for what he called "negative capability" (1817). Its root, I think, lies in the capacity to accept and tolerate anxiety, then to learn from it rather than flee it through heavy armaments of defense that demand certainty and control. By contrast, the urgency to know-for-certain derives from the need to quell one's own anxiety. "Negative capability" begins with an *accepting* and *welcoming* of not knowing. It permits an attitude of curiosity and wonder that is nourished by freshness. With it, I can learn something new. I am always surprised by where a poem takes me and how a poem ends: "So, THAT journey was where the path was taking me."

I learned from Keats, and from psychoanalyst W.R. Bion who drew heavily from him, that not-knowing is the most vital starting point and presence throughout attempts to make sense of anyone or anything. Bion maintained that a good analyst's approach to working with a patient was to have an inquisitive presence, "without memory or desire." I hope I bring at least some of that to my own poetry-writing (or rather, its writing of me!).

To abide with the capacity of not needing to know is to stand with awe, wonder, compassion, and Being Present – to maintain one's footing in the storm of chaos, to endure terror and be curious about it, to hold onto bizarre experiences and emotions that "you could not make up." It is to discover the path to where I needed to go, on the way to where I thought I was and should be going – to find a quiet place, a sanctuary, amid the Furies. As T.S. Eliot wrote in "Little Gidding" in his *Four Quartets* (1943), "We shall not cease from exploration, and the end of all our exploring will be to arrive where we started and know the place for the first time."

Even amid political and cultural chaos, there are moments and places of refuge and reprieve – and grace. In this book, poems that evoke and bear witness to the relentless story line of the dark side of human nature, are punctuated by poems that have offered me a tincture of grace and even of hope that we might redeem ourselves from our self-destructiveness. A clump of dainty buttercups amid a cacophony of mowed weeds in unwelcoming soil, does not redeem the wasteland of the human spirit and body in the Age of Trump, the Age of COVID-19, with its worsening mutations, and the brutal Russian invasion of Ukraine in February 2022. Gratitude and wonder do not dispel terror and despair, but still, they are to be treasured.

It is my hope that the poems of *Standing in the Chaos* will not only share with you my inner, outer, and relational worlds, but will resonate with *your own* life, and give you deeper access to it and to making sense of it.

Howard F. Stein,
Oklahoma City, OK, US
January 2024

Poems

Body Language

The photograph seized me;
My frozen eyes could only stare at it –
A man's outstretched, brown-skinned
Arm, reached as far as it could
Upward toward the side of
An old yellow bus, door now closed,
Bursting with people from El Salvador,
Honduras, and Guatemala,
Fleeing vigilante militias,
Marauding street gangs,
Who would shoot any one
They chose to – in night raids,
In daylight and no place to hide.

The rickety bus was headed
Northward across Mexico
To the southern border
With the United States,
Refugees from terror,
Seeking escape, asylum,
Safety, hope, home....

The open palm of the man's
Splayed hand pressed hard
Against a closed window
Of the bus, as if to cling –
His frightened plea,
His final defiant protest
Before the bus pulled out.
Losing his footing, he fell, sobbing,
To the parched ground.
The driver would not wait,
Maybe could not.
Perhaps there was no room
For even one more.

Who is the more fortunate –
The desolate, haggard man
Left behind, or the hapless
And hopeful people on the bus,
Facing a long, slow, hot, sweaty ride,
Who chose to flee death
For unwelcome
At the closed
Gates of hope?

Four Haiku

Dry earth caked and cracked
This drought could last forever
Gratitude for rain.

Have you seen my mom?
Our borders are not secure.
We are all afraid.

Dickinson was right.
Hope's feathers are very light.
Birds on the feeder.

Anniversary
November 9, *Kristallnacht*
The old fear returns

Coronavirus (COVID-19) 2020, or the Natural History of Disease.

Coronavirus 2020, world-wide pandemic,
Called natural disaster, animal-human transfer,
Perhaps in China but as old as the Agricultural Revolution,
When people settled in towns and cities,
Groups large enough for infectious disease
To spread like an open prairie grass fire.
Natural history of disease – like I learned in fifth grade.

Who would think we humans are part
Of nature that shapes the course of nature?
Consider Donald J. Trump, Presidential Oracle
Of the United States, who, like Wagner's Norns,
Foretells because he is all-knowing.
Our presidential oracle possesses unprecedented power
To know the truth and impose it.

So with the coronavirus plague, that seemed to begin
Its dread journey of sickness and death
In Wuhan, China, in late 2019.
For some two and a half months,
Our presidential oracle knew better
Than to heed earlier warnings about the certainty of a pandemic.
He wrote off any imminent danger. This virus was just like

Ordinary flu and would quickly pass, he assured us.
With the sweep of a pen, he dismissed
Cadres of public health experts abroad
And from his closest councils here.
I'm a businessman, he reminded us:
Who needs to pay so many people
To sit around and do nothing?

Dams everywhere began to burst;
Our presidential oracle noticed only the trickle.
When he at last acknowledged the grave danger,
Its cause was everyone else's fault: a plot
By his political foes to defeat him. He called
The pandemic, "The Chinese Virus," *theirs*,
As though they inflicted it on us.
The presidential oracle, great builder of walls,
Unwittingly left our door open
And let the pestilence in.

Who knows how many
tens of thousands of people
Would become gravely ill and die
Because our presidential oracle believed only himself?
Surely, I am more infallible than any science!

If the presidential oracle
Has shaped part of the history
Of the disease, how entirely natural, then,
Is the history of the coronavirus?

Sometimes, natural history
Of disease is not entirely natural.
The prairie fire is already there –
We supply the gasoline and ignition.

Train Ride

Ready for my trip
I walked to the train station
With my two suitcases
To buy a ticket
I asked the stationmaster
To put me in the sleeper car
I don't rest well sitting up
He gave me a slight smile
Pointed me to the cars
Far down the track
Took one of my suitcases
Saying I could only take one
That in any event
I wouldn't need two
For where I was going
He added once more
With that same winsome smile
You may have a little wait
But rest assured
The train will not depart
Without you

Condolences Post Mortem

Dad died at 94, after a fall,
A broken pelvis, and a short illness.
Job's advisors streamed by
The grieving family —
"He looks so good in the open casket";
"He lived to a ripe old age";
"Be grateful you had him so long";
"He lived a full life right to the end";
"He's in a better place now";
"He's no longer suffering."
Such well-intentioned reassurances
Did not reassure us —
Though they might have reassured
The ones who were speaking.
I was a screen for their platitudes.
We were not greedy with Dad's life;
It's just that there is never enough time.
Dying is still living, alive,
Here in this place.

Death is the slamming of a heavy door
In the face. Then you hear
The lock close behind the door.
There is no undoing that cavernous crash.
I found myself comforting Job's comforters
That their words were adequate to the task.
I could not bring myself to tell them
They had only made the void more terrible.

Moments of Connection

There are moments of connection
In this living sea of desolation.

I am on the North American Great Plains,
Paying for my pizza to two dark-skinned
Young men. "Are you from here?"
One asked me. What would I reply —
To them, even to myself?
"I'm originally from Pittsburgh, but
I've lived here nearly 32 years."
So where am I from, I silently asked myself.
With full beard and *kippah*
I didn't look like I was
From here. To whom
Did I just give myself away?

The second one asks me, I suppose
While glancing at the *kippah** on my head,
"Do you speak Hebrew? I wondered
Who these two were. What dare I say?
I finally broke my silence:
"A little, mostly Hebrew to pray."

---

* Jewish skull cap, a sign of respect to G-d

They persisted, *"Mah schlomchah?"**
One asked. I replied without even
Thinking, *"Ha Kol ba Seder,"***
Though all was not really right
With me. Was I on trial, or
Were they attempting to make
Contact with me
At some place deeper than
The thickness of pizza cheese?
I had passed some unstated test;
I was no longer foreign.

They beamed at my response.
"We're from Jerusalem."
I didn't ask which part.
I relaxed, feeling now strangely at home,
Having just felt like an alien
Though this was my country.
"We hope you come back soon,"
They said as I left. Perhaps,
Just perhaps, they were
Glad to see me as well as
My money.

---

* "How are you?"
** "I'm fine." (literally, "' (literally, "Everything is in order.")

Two Crossings

I crossed
The river
And took the bridge
With me.

    Faith enforced
    Left no room for doubt

Later, I crossed
The bridge
And took the river
With me.

    Doubt let loose
    Left room for faith

"'Who's on First./?' Revisited"*

What if...
Bud Abbott and Lou Costello's
Vaudeville comedy routine,
"Who's on first./?",
Was taken as serious stuff
That drives you crazy –
Nothing comical about it.

"Who's on first." –
Is it a question, or an observation,
About a first baseman in baseball?
Neither Abbott nor Costello
Can – or will –
Hear the distinction,
Or at least acknowledge
Any ambiguity. Abbott,
the straight man,
Can only restate his position,

---

* Who's on First./?" was first performed in a comedy routine in the touring Vaudeville review, Hollywood Bandwagon, in 1937. Its subject is an attempt to identify the names of the players in their positions on a baseball field. Continuously revised, improvised, copyrighted in 1944, translated into many languages, the comedy routine's message and enactment are understood widely, if not universally, as closely resembling one's own experience. (https://en.wikipedia.org/wiki/Who%27s_on_First%3F#History (Accessed 8/11/19). Here is a link to an actual 1953 performance: https://www.youtube.com/watch?v=kTcRRaXV-fg (Accessed 1/21/2020).

While Costello, excitable, volatile,
Goes crazy in his confusion.

When did angle
Become fact,
Digging in one's heels,
The only way
To settle a dispute?

When two people,
Or groups, or nations,
Cannot, will not, listen to the other,
They hear only echoes
Of their own voices –
Intransigence spawns
Frozen misunderstanding;
Headstrong certainty
Reappears as irrefutable fact.

"Who's on first./?" –
Interrogative or declarative?
Inflection should have the final say,
Seems so obvious.
Dare I imagine hearing it
The way you hear it?

Asking you how you hear it?
Certainly not!
I could Lose my footing.
Exasperation soars because
So much is at stake
In being right –
In convincing others
There is only
One way of understanding.

The argument could
Go on forever,
Each escalating round,
Louder and louder,
Ever-more desperate.

Humpty Dumpty's Needless Fall[*]

Modern version of children's nursery rhyme: *Humpty Dumpty sat on a wall,/ Humpty Dumpty had a great fall;/ All the king's horses and all the king's men,/ Couldn't put Humpty together again.*

Humpty Dumpty, that hapless egg,
Sustained a preventable fall.
If all the King's horses
And the King's men who rode on them,
Had been up on the ledge with Humpty,
They would have immediately noticed
How precarious his standing.
As he inched closer toward the edge,
They could have called out in alarm
While they enclosed him with their arms,
Rescued him from his ineptitude.
But no! They waited safely below,
Stood by, watched him helplessly,
As he lost footing, tumbled,
Then shattered in a thousand shards.

---

[*] Historical Note:
https://en.wikipedia.org/wiki/Humpty_Dumpty#Origins Accessed 8/10/19.
"The first known publication of Humpty Dumpty was included in *Juvenile Amusements* by Samuel Arnold in 1797. In that version, the last lines read "Fourscore men and fourscore more / could not make Humpty Dumpty where he was before." Over the next century, the rhyme appeared in numerous books with variations on the lyrics."

In their doleful lamentation,
They consoled themselves in one voice:
"Humpty should have been more cautious!"

The Second Flood

Signs, abundant signs, all unheeded,
Advance warnings by scientists of every stripe,
Unlikeliest prophets with their vast granaries of data:
Warming oceans, melting polar ice,
Methane released from thawing permafrost,
Dying coral reefs, perishing species,
Accelerated mining and burning petroleum and coal
From insatiable humans and their
Fossil-fuel-devouring machines.

Year upon year, waters rose, continued to rise,
First engulfed helpless islands
In every sea, ate away at shore-lines
Of every continent, made their way inland,
Poisoned groundwater with saltwater.
All life on the shrinking continents
Withdrew further inland, encroaching
Upon one another. Species after species perished.
Even remaining land was no sanctuary:
Deadlier thunderstorms; mammoth tornadoes;
Monstrous hurricanes; more inundating river-floods;
Longer, expansive droughts –
And still ocean waters rose,
Sea claiming land, salt water triumphant.

We called it The Second Flood.
Long ago, the Bible story tells,
G-d's wrath at human wickedness
Led Him to destroy all life,
Except for righteous Noah
And two land animals
Of every kind aboard the Ark.
Afterward even G-d realized
That this time He had gone too far,
And vowed never again
To flood the earth.
From His somewhere-perch, G-d,
Helpless in His Heaven,
Watched destiny unfold,
Unable to halt and reverse
What He did not first inflict.

This time, it was *our* flood,
Not G-d's. And no,
Unlike G-d, we did not repent
Of our deed. Audacity spurned remorse –
We dared the earth even more,
Combustion engines humming,
Burning, spewing, poisoning air –
Until even they were
Swallowed up by the rising sea.

Backlighting in Autumn

Long-forgotten chill
And diminishing sun
Perform their natural alchemy
On deciduous trees,
Transmute dark green
Scrub oak leaves
Into yellows, oranges,
Golds, and ruddy browns.
These scrawny survivors
Wring from hardscrabble lives
A severe kind of beauty.

Backlit by a fading sun,
A patch of glowing leaves
Lingers before nightfall,
Suspended in the air
As much as in time,
Then vanishes until morning –
Minus a few more leaves –
Backlit now by an eastern sun.

Wonders of the world
Come in small sizes,
Magnificence, not
A matter of scale,
But of wakeful
Eyes' recognition
Of what soon passes
From sight.

Exile, a Montage of Voices

Who will hear? Who will listen?
Who will let us in?
Who will not discard us?
Who can be at home in a world in which
everything is bought and sold
as real estate?
Who speaks for the evicted and disinherited?
Who says: come dwell with us?
Share our bread? Share our wine?

No place to go; no place to stay,
we live as characters in Chagall paintings –
we drift in the air and wander on the ground.
We live the terror of Picasso's *Guernica*.
We are condemned to be strangers
wherever we go.
We are No-Where, belong in No-Place;
no one claims us; they strew us like waste.
We are drifters who knock on locked doors.
No Irish – Jews, Catholics, Slovaks, Poles,
Italians, Okies, Japanese, Vietnamese, Latinos,
Blacks, Muslims, Somalis, Africans, Haitians,
Gays, Lesbians, Trans-sexuals – *need apply*.

* * *

We don't care where you go or if you die,
we just don't want you here.
You are not hapless refugees fleeing death,
But vile invaders of our pure but mortal bodies.
You bring death to us
in the guise of seeking shelter.
Our borders are our skin;
you have penetrated under our skin
and must be cut out because you poison.
You have made us sick and weak; you are our disease,
and ridding ourselves of you is our cure.
Do you wish us die?
Have you no mercy?
Our dreams gyre down into nightmares.

We fear you; therefore we hate you;
therefore we spurn you and cast you out.
Wretched refuse, go back to your teeming shores.
Not pity, but disdain, is ours for you
who dream of open doors.
Our home is not your home,
and will never be.

Our hard edges greet you to keep you out:
walls, fences, doors, barricades, barbed wire,
forbiddingly uniformed border police.
We offer no soft beds for you to rest on.
Our land is no sanctuary for the weary,
but a fortress for the strong.

Go, just go; die, just die.
Stay away; go away.
You are not *Our Kind*.

* * *

Curses and prayers.
Fists and tears.
Threats and entreaties.
Above all, no mercy.

Coalescences

It was not love at first sight —
The main theme stated outright,
Unmistakable from the start.
No, it was hardly discernable
In old-fashioned correspondence,
Letters written on stationery
And mailed across half a continent.

Themes out of the news coalesced
Of our long and busy lives
From bits and pieces of thematic material
Like the beginning of Beethoven's Ninth Symphony,
From fragments of chaos
To the full-blown subject
That could never have been guessed.

Old Pickup

I saw an old pickup truck today –
in mint condition for all its years.
I couldn't guess its age.
I only know that I was young
when it was new.

Sinking In

A single autumn does not suffice
For me to grasp the weight
This time of year bears for me.
I can fee! its freight long before
I have words to give to it.

Each new autumn is the place
Zum Raum wird hier die Zeit
(Where Time here becomes Space*),
Allusion as much as season.
How many cycles of
Decline and decay
Must I witness before
The lesson of impermanence
At last sinks in?

---

* Richard Wagner, *Parsifal.*

What does a deep green
Post oak leaf
In the fullness of summer
Know about losing its chlorophyll
Only a few months ahead,
Then dropping, limp and lifeless,
To the ground?

Astronomers say there are
Trillions of planets out there,
That to claim our tiny
Earth To be a singularity
Is to indulge In self-deception.
Yet this negligible speck
Is the cherished home
I hope never to leave.

Walk to the Polling Place, November 2020, US

Aerosolized droplets
Of hate and dread
Comingle with the coronavirus,*
Infect and kill where they will,
No one invulnerable to their stealth.

A thick miasma has settled upon
This line of hopefuls who are here
To do their part
In choosing the next tribal chief,
No one certain to be alive
The day of his inauguration.

Some wear face masks,
Others renounce protection,
Some keep distance
From persons in front and behind them,
Others crowd, flaunt the rules.
Fear and bravado,
In common determination
To cast a prized vote.

---

* Coronavirus, or COVID-19, worldwide pandemic, 2020

So much time to wait,
And yet too much time for
Questions to seep into
Contemplation of
The main reason to be here,
To decide for whom to vote –
Questions never before asked:

Who among us will not be
In line for the next election,
Taken by the plague instead?
Who could be here now
But is not, because of
Some exclusionary law?

Do voting machines record my choices,
shape the future,
Or is the outcome already determined?
Are there secrets no one will reveal?
Doubt swells: For what do I
Stand so long In line and wait?

What future do the witches
In Shakespeare's *Macbeth* foretell?
Toward what fate do Wagner's Norns
Weave their rope to cast their spell? –
Or are their auguries owned as well?

Mired in a smog of doubt,
I still refuse to leave;
When at last I arrive
In the polling booth,
I cast my vote –
And pretend it matters.

"Not 'Either/Or,' but 'Both/And'"

Insatiable maw, coronavirus pandemic,
Arrived December 2019,
Still raging, March 2021;
New vaccines, over a half-million dead.

A thin layer of frost at sunrise
Glistens on rooftops. Fleeting diamonds –
Does rapid evaporation increase their worth?

Hospitals bulge, often burst,
With masses of sick people.
New diagnoses and treatments
Cannot keep up with new infections.
Improvisation never ends.
Daily updates of statistics –
One person dies at a time.

A family of foxes takes up residence
In the wide culvert beneath my driveway;
Drainage pipe, a place called home.
Neighbors now.

Toxic miasma, stringent precautions,
Flaunted medical warnings
To wear facial masks,
Keep six feet apart, wash hands.
The monster stalks its prey,
We dare it to strike.

     White, broad-winged gulls
     Float far overhead,
     Glow in the evening sun,
     Gather soon at a nearby lake
     To rest together
     In one another's company.

Doctors and nurses
Work long shifts,
Keep working despite exhaustion;
Many die from the infection
That consumes those they treat.

     The neighborhood turkey wobbles
     Every few weeks into
     Our back yard – and everyone's
     In this part of town.
     What matter fences to this turkey
     Whom we have adopted
     And who has adopted us?

41

People in health professions
Work obliviously unrecognized
For their devotion –
Never enough medical supplies,
Never enough room, never enough time –
Still, they press on:
They form the resistance.

Scattered streetlights and house lights,
Lanterns of reassurance,
Night watchmen in winter's gloom,
On a canvas Edward Hopper
Could have painted.
They help us navigate
Through the peril.

Fresh corpses, refrigerated in lines of trucks;
Medical training offered no preparation
For swamps like this. Lifeless words like
"Mass casualties" fail to tell
The story of what it is like
To live amid this siege.

Scrub oak and post oak
Sprout delicate pastel green leaves —
Who can imagine spring
After the most destructive ice storm
And the longest strangulating
Siberian winter siege
In written history?
Incredulous spring,
Intrepid spring;

Not either/or,
But both/and;
Stillness...

Linguistics Lesson, or, Making a List and Checking It Twice

"...I shall go on writing. That is my heroism. I will bear witness, precise witness."

"It's not the big things that are important to me, but the everyday life of tyranny which gets forgotten. A thousand mosquito bites are worse than a blow to the head. I observe, note down the mosquito bites."

—Victor Klemperer. *I Will Bear Witness: 1942–1945, A Diary of the Nazi Years.* Random House/ The Modern Library, New York, 2001, p. 61 & pp. 307–308.

Whispers, shouts,
In language supposed to be
Foreign to this place,
Excluded and banished –

> Totalitarianism
>
> Fascism
>
> Terrorism
>
> Anti-Semitism
>
> White Nationalism
>
> Racism
>
> George Orwell's 1984 *Newspeak*

Accompanying these, are

Straggling lines of fleeing refugees,
    Called "invaders," rapists, and drug smugglers
No longer human beings and members of "huddled masses,"
    But insects and viruses
New laws that codify hate
Cleansing government raids and seizures
Children locked in cages "like animals"
Families separated and infants lost to the bureaucracy
Massive barriers
Made of steel
    Of hardened hearts
    Expulsions
Deportations
Disappearances
Targets on their backs

You can't make it up –
But still you wonder if you
Are imagining things.
You think of the "power of words,"
But then feel the fist-punch
Of "Words of Power,"
Where truth is fake and fake is truth,
And "Speak Truth to Power"

Turns into "Speak Power to Truth,"
Reality is what Our Leader
And his Base say it is,
Loyally "reported" by Fox News and AM Radio

We are beaten numb and weary
By daily news on TV, radio,
Newspapers, Internet, social media,
Presidential tweets,
Government pronouncements,
And Our Leader's
Reality-altering Newspeak

State Terror has succeeded
Beyond the right's fondest hopes.
We have installed them in the inner spaces:

The idea of white nationalists
As domestic terrorists
Is a cruel fiction;
Only Muslims, Hispanics, Socialists,
Democrats are – none of these
Us, but Them.
Projection rules us
By day and by night.

Drops of water,
One by one,
Upon a rock,
Imperceptibly wear it down,
Make a hollow
Where there had been
Solid stone.
Even a rock can
Become exhausted.

Franz Kafka would find
A familiar world here,
Everywhere he encountered his
Torture apparatus
From In the Penal Colony.
The Apparatus inscribes
Greatness into the backs
Of all the souls it executes.
The machine's needles
Can etch anyone it suspects
Of failing to make American white again.

Even two plus two
No longer equal four;
Nothing much adds up
Anymore.
No difference, too, between

The seven days of the week:
Long named Monday, Tuesday,
Wednesday, Thursday, Friday,
Saturday, Sunday,
Every day has become None Day.
The Great Leader now rules time.

We no longer live in fear;
Each day we Live The Fear.
It is a living Presence
Who dwells among us,
Stalks and occupies
Our cells and our souls.
We are its subjects.

References:

Chua, A. & Rubenfeld, J. (2018). "The threat of tribalism." *The Atlantic*. Vol. 322, 3 October 2018.

Lupton, R., Myers, W. & Thornton, J. (2017); "Republicans are the party of ideological inconsistency." *Washington Post*, 2 October, https://www.washingtonpost.com/news/monkey-cage/.

Hochschild, A. (2018). *Strangers in their own land: Anger and mourning on the American right*. [Kindle Edition]. New York: The New Press.

https://www.yahoo.com/news/trumps-rushmore-trip-draws-real-041930807.html

Allcorn, Seth. (2020). "Cultures of Grievance: Creating Polarization from Chosen Traumas." *The Journal of Psychohistory*. 48(1) Summer 2020: 23–40.

Allcorn, Seth and Stein, Howard F. (2018). "Donald Trump, Empty Vessel and Sum of all Projections." *The Journal of Psychohistory*. 46(1)Summer 2018: 2–16.

Stein, Howard F. and Allcorn, Seth. (2018). "A Fateful Convergence Animosity Toward Obamacare, Hatred of Obama, the Rise of Donald Trump, and Overt Racism in America." *The Journal of Psychohistory*. 45(4) Spring 2018: 234–243.

Allcorn, Seth. (2020). "Sentience In Contemporary Conservative American Politics." *The Journal of Psychohistory*. 47(4) Spring 2020: 276–292.

https://www.nytimes.com/2020/05/23/opinion/sunday/trump-mask-coronavirus.html?action=click&module=Opinion&pgtype=Homepage .

Scrub Oak Branches in Winter's Night

Scrub oak branches bereft of leaves,
Naked bark, their protective skin,
Survival is a dare against
Invasion by wind, ice, and snow.
Their hope is to wait and outlast.

Absence is where all winters lead.

Amid this remorseless danger,
A tiny reprieve from peril:
Through these branches I see the sky.

The Race

But at my back I always hear...
—Andrew Marvell

Eager to run,
The horses line up
At the starting gate,
Hardly able to wait.
Each horse bears a name—
Acute or chronic,
Physical or mental,
Terminal or treatable,
They are beyond ready—
The timer fires his starting gun;
Impatient horses take off down the track,
Press their way toward the goal.
Soon the co-morbidities
Round the bend,
Then head into the final stretch,
Neck and neck.
COPD, AFib, Parkinson's, and the rest—
All give it their best.
It is anyone's guess
Who will cross the finishing line first,
Win the race,
And claim the coveted prize.

For Now...

The tumor is out;
the surgeon got it all.
CT-scan and blood work
are clear: no trace of cancer –
for now. But this is
the kind of cancer that
often recurs within the first two years,
then must be monitored
for a lifetime.

So, how long does for now last?
This is my son we are talking about:
Don't give me probabilities.
He's still a kid: Will he have a life?

Now for the bi-monthly
trek to the big city
for the solemn ritual
of CT-scan, blood work,
and feeling his lymph nodes –
to get it early, if it comes back.

For now, a sigh of relief –
a wary sigh —
lest we get caught off guard
like we were the first time;
the second time will be worse.

Live your life, the doctors say,
and don't look too often
into the rearview mirror.
So, with double vision,
we return to life –
for now.

What Is a Door?

passageway
barrier
surface
statement
setting for stories
and great drama –

like the time a hapless manager
fled the executive's office sobbing,
when he had taken his boss's
"open door policy" at his word,
and came by to voice a concern –

or like the time my intimidated mother
pounded on the door of our apartment's
single bathroom where her ten year-old son
was sitting on the toilet. "You better come out.
Your father is waiting to go in. You know
you'll be in big trouble if you don't finish
and flush now!" –

or like the time apartment doors
were called upon to serve as exclamation points
to my parents' frequent and escalating arguments.
If my memory is correct, mom and dad always
slammed two solid wood doors, one each,
and the whole apartment shook in fear.

A door is
no simple thing.

Our Lives in Silos – For Michael A. Diamond and Seth Allcorn.

Silos –
A single shape
First comes to mind –
In farmland and their towns;
Tall, cylindrical elevators
That store grain;
At work, towering silos store people,
Layer upon layer,
Corporate sileage
Called employees –

Vertical and horizontal silos,
Departments, divisions, units
On stacked floors,
Or sprawled across a single floor,
Divided by walls and minds,
Partitions visible and invisible –
In the same building;
In separate buildings
Across the city,
The country, the ocean.

Silo thinking –
Where we begin and end,
What we do,
Who we are.
We defend our silos
As if our lives
Depended on them.
We are *Here*; *You* are *There*.
Space, skin, boundaries.

If we cannot touch their surfaces
With our fingers,
We can touch them
With our minds.

Silos enclose and comfort us;
Silos imprison us –
Straitjacket our bodies and our minds,
Reassure us with their rigidity.

The same dissonant conversation
Can be heard within and between silos everywhere;
Cries of injustice engulf the place:

> *Research* complains,
> *Finance* never gives us
> Enough money to operate.

Finance protests,
Research, Shipping, Purchasing,
Sales whine at us
That we're withholding
From *them*, but are generous
With money to other divisions,
That we're playing favorites.
Sales accuses *Administration*
Of getting all the perks,
While *Sales* only receives
Leftovers.
They favor the others;
They neglect us.
We get put in the basement;
They get the good locations
And so much else.

Corporate tribes –
Our walls nourish
And defend
Our identities,
Borders impermeable,
Ancient Us/Them at work,

Monoliths –
We are the stone.

Streetlight in Winter

Outside my bedroom window
A solitary lamppost
Pierces winter's long darkness.
Scrub oaks' barren trunks
And bony branches
Carve a stark silhouette
Against a blinding white sky
That oozes with foreboding
Amid the eerie stillness
Of this winter night.

Am I watchman of Dunsinane castle?
At my window, do I see Birnam Wood*
Advance toward my hill and home?
Do scarecrow trees, their
Scrawny arms outstretched,
Approach unopposed?

---

* The image comes from Act 5 of *Macbeth*, by William Shakespeare, in which Malcom's (the murdered Duncan's son) army surreptitiously closes in on Macbeth's castle by camouflaging themselves with tree branches they hold before them.

As the apparition closes in,
The soft glow of the mute street light
Alone gives me balm.
Together, we will prevail
Through the treacherous night.

Mind Tricks

Beneath a stand of scrub oak
I look upward – adolescent leaves,
Pastel green, still supple;
Translucent in late afternoon sun,
They seem to radiate
Their own delicate light,
Summer too far off to be in sight.
Only a month ago,
Still-bare branches,
Imprisoned by winter,
Pierced the arctic air
Like witches' gaunt fingers.
Yet – how could this be?
Wrapped now in spring's
Luxuriant new abundance,
I strain to recall
Winter's barren breast
And fleeting light.
As I stand enveloped
Inside the cocoon
Of spring's lush garden,
Winter is not possibility
Let alone inevitability –
Yearning's urgency is enough
To banish winter forever.

Love's Decorum

The centerpiece is a soup bowl
Atop a spotless plate, then
To their upper left a butter dish.
In front of the plate,
A lustrous drinking glass,
A crisp cloth napkin inside,
Opening like a flower.
To the right of the plate, a knife
And two spoons, the closer, and larger,
For soup; the farther, a teaspoon, for coffee.
Between the plate and glass, a dessert spoon,
Perfectly perpendicular to the other utensils.
Every place setting at the table is identical.

Impeccable logic, this
Domestic mealtime geometry,
A perfect marriage,
Everything in its place –
As if to stray a single spoon
Would betray the entire show.

Appearance is all –
"Where once was love,
There shall decorum be."*

---

* I have taken poetic license with Sigmund Freud's famous dictum, "Where id is, there shall ego be." From *New Introductory Lectures on Psychoanalysis*, 1932.

Coffee Cup

You, with your coffee cup
securely in your hand,
tell me that you keep
seeing me in the hallway
with a cup in my hand,
either empty or full, and
Didn't I have anything
better to do with my time?
I decline to reply.

Landscape and Dreamscape, Ghost Ranch, N.M. (a prose poem)

High desert, northern New Mexico – where you can touch metaphors, and they return as visible landscape; where massive sandstone mesas and shining cliffs hint that space is parable for time, and time is medium for space; where over 200 million years of fossil history chant hymns and tell stories of life long ago; where aged cottonwood and ponderosa pine dwell happily among the long-dead but still firmly planted skeletons of mesquite and juniper; where remnants of an ancient inland sea sing graceful *bel canto* to the text of today's scorching summer sun and bone-dry stream beds.

What sort of landscape is this – where you can touch metaphors in buttes; where everything firm is allusion; where figures of speech usher forth from the yellow flowers of the hardy Chamisa; where boundless sky that encloses the badlands, opens lungs for deep breathing, and eyes for deep seeing?

Am I seeing? Am I dreaming? Must I choose? If mesas and pinnacles are vast painted canvases on my soul, are my words Ekphrastic script on a Mobius strip, where high desert and its indwelling presence undulate seamlessly on a single surface; where at one moment a deep gorge is geology and geography, in the next moment pigment and brush, then back again; where doxology incarnates time as it assumes the form of Bach fugue and *Magnificat – Sicut erat in principio, et nunc, et semper, et in saecula saeculorum.* Amen.*

In these badlands, call and response resonate, amplify each other, become each other – poem as world, world as poem, at once impossible and manifest, landscape and dreamscape continuous, on this Mobius strip of life.

---

* "As it was in the beginning, and (is) now, and forever shall be, world without end. Amen." (from *Gloria Patri*)

Masks and Eyes

Faces bifurcated
By two plagues entwined,
COVID-19 and the Age of Trump –
Lower parts of the face
Covered by polyethylene
Or cellulose medical grade,
Now KN95, thanks
To Omicron mutation –
Even high fashion cloth;
Face masks, that
Protect and conceal
More or less
Half a human face –
Nearly one's entire nose,
Mouth, chin, and
Most of the side of
A person's face,
All expression hidden –

Except for eyes,
That reveal the truth
And give away
The heart.

Difference, a Riddle for the Age of COVID-19

What is the difference
Between
A visiting nurse
And a
Visiting hearse?

A hearse only
Visits once.

Drought

Calamitous drought
Act of Nature, Act of G-d –

Over-grazed, over-plowed,
Over-planted, over worked,
No day of Sabbath, no time for rest.

We are the sorcerer
Who curses our fields.

Riot of Roses

Is this riot of roses
A sign of G-d's repentance
For last October's ice storm
That paralyzed the city,
Split trees like celery stalks,
Snapped branches from ice's weight;
Followed in February
By a Siberian siege
Of bitter cold and more ice
That wrecked an entire region's
Electrical grid, with death
And dread chaos in its wake?
Punishment? Meaninglessness?

What kind of sense can I make
Of miles of disfigured trees,
That bled their pain into earth?
A Darwinian struggle?
How many times have I asked:
"Where was G-d when…?", and waited
In silence and despair for
An answer that never came?

Is my riot of roses
A paltry consolation
From somewhere or from someone
To persuade me that beauty
And horror are some cosmic
Balancing act that takes turns
In inflicting grief and then
Offering salve for its wounds?
Or is this island of grace
A joke without a joker?
My endless stream of questions
Offers no relief to my
Frightened, erratic heartbeat.
Questions have become my trap.
Solutions are now problems.
Spring is when all roses bloom.
No mystery about this.

Seeing my unhappiness,
My roses try to speak now....
"Sit with us, and breathe with us;
Look closely at our petals –
Try to see far *into them.*
Go where they wish to take you –
It is a place behind us
No one can see, only sense.
You speak the wrong language here.

Here you will not find answers;
Here you will not find logic.
But here you will find our G-d –
And you will find gratitude,
Not only that we exist
And have bloomed again after
So much peril, but also
That your eyes can recognize
New life after so much death."

Native Wit

Not for lack of native wit
Have cottonwoods prevailed
Upon prairie's crusted skin.

Brief torrents of summer rain
Fill dry streambeds, soon
Give way to months of drought.

Crocus, tulip, pom-pom, azalea,
Forsythia; redbud – they take their
Chances with Spring's early dare.

When, for blooming, nothing else
Remains – enter cottonwoods,
Hearty laggards of the plains.

Whitman's Miracles, Further Evidence

For Phil Floyd

"As to me I know of nothing else but miracles...."
Walt Whitman, "Miracles." (1856/ evised 1881)

On my short morning walk to the mailbox,
A patch of tiny buttercups (*Ranunculus*)
Steals my vision –
Five yellow petals arrayed on each stalk,
Baby-skin soft, stand scarcely
Above the cacophony of grasses
And other green leafy
Plants of robust biodiversity.
What an ecological niche,
This odd neighborhood of immigrants,
Chance meetings,
Thrown together by the wind,
There to greet me through the summer.
Who dare call these
Miniature miracles weeds?

My parcel of buttercups
Comforts me in its
Utter unlikelihood –
Miracle of fulfillment

Of a dream I never had
Or knew I wished to have.

My filing cabinet drawers
Cannot rescue me here.
Explanations they have accumulated
And store to overflow
Fail the questions
This place poses to me –
How to stand still
In amazement and wonder?

***

Only a few steps
From my buttercups,
I open my hand wide,
Spread my palm and fingers
Upon the curve of rugged,
Deep-furrowed bark
Of my post oak tree (*Quercus stellata*).
Touch first feels
What my mind eventually
Finds words for.

When my fingers explore
This harsh, craggy surface,
They do not discern
Some entity called *wood*;
This bark lives,
Tough-skinned guardian
Of rising sap to distant leaves,
Not here future lumber
Or chopped-up firewood.

My hand discerns a miracle –
My mind only slowly
Grasps what my hand
Already knows.

Keeping Time

Wall clocks
Floor clocks
Table clocks
Tenor tick
Bass tick
Snare drum
Kettle drum
Cymbals
Gong
Chatter
Heavy footfalls
Steady pulse
Metronomic stroke
Pianissimo
Fortissimo
Rapturous klang

Throbbing din
Steady pulse
Time's heartbeat

Then
As if obeying
Some peremptory command
All clocks cease ticking
In unison
Fall lifeless to the floor
Their hands stiff in rigor mortis
Their gears locked in cardiac arrest
Their faces frozen in fixed stare

Still as a corpse
All the clocks have
Run out of time

Chaos Theory

Everything here in its place —
Company vision, mission statement,
Goals and objectives, strategic plan,
Procedures manual, organizational chart....
To our ship's captain and navigator —
The CEO on the bridge,
His, a perfect view
Of everything below —
We are steady and right on course.

Our leader's daily barrage
Of caustic e-mails and memoranda
Catches everyone off guard.
He fires off scathing messages,
Threatens reprimands, demotions,
Even firings for employees who
Fail to carry out his orders,
Who do not live up to his expectations,
Or who disagree with his policies.
For a drastic change he decrees one day,
He often hurls a contradictory directive the next —
Life here, an endless scramble.

The entire company has become
A concatenation of fire brigades
Who rush in their engines
All around town
To put out fire after fire,
Never knowing when or where
Our CEO might set the next one –
Alongside the jobs for which
We are paid,
Our primary task is
To survive this helter skelter –
Starting fires, putting out fires,
The rhythm to which
Our company's heart beats.
We live life one fire at a time,
Each fire station responding to its own fire,
As though unconnected to the others.

We keep a log
Of each fire we extinguish,
Knowing all along the arsonist
Is unfinished with his mischief.
We carefully study each blaze
To determine its specific cause,
While anticipating the next,

We know we cannot prevent,
Vigilance and guessing,
Our way of life.

We do not recognize
Our leader's fires are not separate events,
But that Chaos is the secret combustion
He sets upon us in each blaze.
The Chief Executive Officer of this vast business
Is the Lord of Chaos in disguise.

To maintain his arrogant strut,
He imposes on us his desperation –
His Furies, our Chaos.
From the corner of our eye,
We keep constant watch;
In frightened allegiance with him,
We persuade ourselves
That all is well
With us and our company –
That we are steady
And right on course.

The Old Recliner   In memory of Luke and Leia Stein

My old recliner,
Sanctuary and refuge,
Nesting place,
Worn upholstery, but still soft,
Polyester velour,
Once plush and deep blue –
I never thought of it
As furniture.

I slept there for days
After many surgeries,
And year upon year
Of winter pneumonias –
But never alone, my cat-person Luke,
Companion, comforter, sentinel,
Asleep at my side, or
Upon my undulating chest.
His virtual sister, Leia,
Spitfire daredevil,
Slept on a close-by chair,
Eventually joined us in my lap.

When I was not resting,
My open laptop sat
On my thighs; I tried to work –
They had other ideas.
Sometimes Luke lay content
Between my belly
And the keyboard
While I typed –
Though my long arms had
Limits on how far
They could stretch over him.
As soon as I left the chair,
Luke hopped up, took it over,
Claimed squatter's rights,
Later, eminent domain,
Occupied it for hours, protested
Briefly when I returned,
Hoisted him into my arms,
Lowered him into my lap.
Luke promptly dozed off
As though nothing had changed.

As to whom the recliner belonged,
The possessive "my" remained
A matter of question.
Still through years of property disputes,
Luke, the recliner, and I,

And sometimes Leia, knew
We belonged to each other.
Each morning, Luke was there,
Lying atop the recliner, waiting for me
To open the door from the hall
And welcome me to the day.
They were my compass.

At 16, Luke came down
With kidney disease,
Soon grew gaunt, skeletal,
Listless, ate nothing,
And died. Leia lingered but a year,
Warmed up to me somewhat,
Took blessed naps with me
In now *her* blue recliner,
Mammal comforting mammal –
Then she erupted with the same
Disease that took Luke.
Leia died within a month.

Now, in my study,
The blue recliner has
Only me for company.
It still faces the large window
We three used to look out
Together; it carves a solitary figure

Edward Hopper could have painted.
I sit in the recliner alone –
If I sit there at all.

No more a place –
Just the piece of furniture
It was when it was
First delivered.

Mindfulness

Definition of Insanity: Doing the same thing over and over, expecting different results. (Al-Anon)

Sleepwalk in full sunlight,
Keep the unconscious unconscious,
Repetition compulsion – Who says
It won't work *this* time?
Keen awareness of
Everyone else's flaws,
Though having none of my own
For anyone to notice.

Left turn in
No Left Turn lane
At busy intersection;
Car accident,
Accident on purpose,
Though I'd be
The last one to know.
Why do I so often
Leave home late for meetings,
Then cut corners
To try to make up time?

Practice self-reflection –
Look intensely into
The large frame
That holds no mirror;
Remember daily reading
From Zen books.
Apply wisdom to daily life.
When stressed, take
Long deep breaths,
Take time to let
Your mind wander,
To let go.

Accidentally (again) bang
My head on dryer door while
Focused on doing laundry –
Glasses essential
For my complicated eyes
Fly off my face,
Strike the floor,
Bent out of shape.
In vain I put them
Back on, hoping *this time*
I will still see well,
Only for my vision
To be once more
A blur, while

Intense headache
Follows immediately.
I drive carefully
To my optician
The next day,
Grateful that once again she
Straightens everything,
Restores my sight
To crisp image.
I tell myself,
Next time I do laundry,
I'll be more mindful.

For Whom Do I Say *Kaddish*?*

Tell me, for whom do I say *Kaddish*?
The number grows, so many have died –
My father, my mother, my grandparents,
So many uncles and aunts –
I was named for one, a lifelong soldier
Killed in the Battle of the Bulge;
The millions murdered in death camps,
Including half of my family;
The tens of thousands murdered in pogroms
All over Europe for centuries; the martyred sages.

Then there are the living, the resilient, the survivors,
But whose lives are haunted
By the terrors of so long a history of settling in,
Only to be later hounded out, hunted,
And butchered along the way.
For the tormented living, I say *Kaddish*, too.

---

* The "Mourner's *Kaddish*" is a prayer in Aramaic that Jews recite at appointed places in the Hebrew liturgy for the most part in memory of a deceased relative. For many modern Jews, it might be the only prayer they know. It is recited during the *Yizkor* or memorial service four times a year, twice daily during the eleven-month period of mourning following the death of a family member, and afterwards at the daily services on the anniversary of their death.

I say *Kaddish* even at times
That are not appointed, times
When I am alone and not at the synagogue
In the company of a *minyan.*[*]
I violate the Law to say *Kaddish,*
So many dead, so many names
To remember and to keep alive
In me. Sometimes they take hours
To recite, and I know I will never
Finish. There will always be more.

It slowly creeps into my awareness that
It is my turn to begin to say *Kaddish* for myself –
For hopeless desires, even for hope itself.
For dreams and tasks I have been given
Generations ago and cannot possibly
Fulfil. I gently lay them to rest
In the cemetery of my heart,
And let them finally die with me.

For all these, and more,
I say *Kaddish.*

---

* A *minyan* is a minimum ritual quorum of ten adult Jews, male or female in Conservative and Reform denominations, and only male in Orthodox practice. Any group short of this number cannot perform certain rituals, such as reading the *Torah*, and reciting the *Kaddish*, which are public events.

Sometimes It Is Just What It Is

Sundown, this sundown;
Nightfall, this nightfall;
Before words, these eyes
And memory's eyes.
I do not search for names,
For fast-changing, fast-fading
Colors, as our sun
Glides toward the horizon.

Dying, leave-taking –
Similes and metaphors
Steal the show
From pure immersion –
Sundown is worth
More than its clichés.

Day's end is not my death.
It is *diminuendo*
In earth's rotation.
Crescendo will arrive
In its own time.
Magnificence suffices.

Sometimes, a sunset
That gives me goose bumps
Is just what it is.

A Shirt's Tale

I am a long-sleeved shirt.
I start out my life
Crisply ironed, folded,
Kept in place by cardboard
Sealed in clear plastic wrapping,
Impeccably attired.

A customer purchases me
From a store or by internet
From a distant mail-order house.
He unwraps me, proudly wears me,
Washes and dries me (maybe even irons me),
Hangs me on hangars or puts me in drawers.
Our routine continues for years.
With time, new competitors join the ranks;
Displaced, I lose my seniority
And become just another shirt,
No longer special,
No longer new.

Eventually, my owner
May tire of me,
Wear me less often.
Favor others over me.

If my owner thinks
He can still get a few dollars for me,
He may take me to a thrift store
Like Goodwill and Salvation Army,
Or offer me among other discards
In a garage sale on his driveway.

If he keeps me, eventually I begin
To wear out, wrinkle and fade,
Fray and grow threadbare, even tear.
No one remembers what I was like
When I was young and strong.
My owner might outgrow me,
Gain or lose weight.
I might not fit anymore.

If I manage to survive to old age,
My fate is to be condemned to the rag bag,
To be ripped apart, or cut up into smaller pieces,
Used to dust furniture, to wipe up spills
Of juice or paint or dish water,
To be thrown with other rags
Into the washer, purged of bacteria
With bleach and detergent,
Saved and reused, finally

Tossed into the trash as too stained,
Rank, and useless – my beginnings
As a flawless newborn rarely
Remembered.

My owner, who
Once wore me with pride,
Does not even accord me
A proper funeral.
He ignominiously abandons me
To humiliation and death
In the trash can. Within a week,
Men with their formidable
Garbage truck will haul me away
To the city dump,
Or will incinerate me –
Decay and decomposition
In a common grave;
Ashes in a heap strewn by the wind.

Kelipoth – **Broken Vessels**

After the Jewish Kabbalist Rabbi Isaac Luria of Safed, Israel [1570]

The *breaking of the vessels*:
Amid strewn shards
Of a coronaviral broken universe,
Tiny sparks of light
Gather quietly, unnoticeably,
And cling to the broken shards
Inside the bowls. Divine light
Flows into them for the work
Of *tikkun olam*, the mending
Of the world –
Emanations of Eros,
Making whole through love
What neither plague nor hate
Can dispel.

Into the Vortex

Our spaceship adrift,
No power, no direction,
Caught in a net like a fish,
Struggle to escape
The inescapable.

Imperceptibly at first,
Our ship is drawn into an invisible vortex;
Its downward spiral grows narrower,
Centripetal speed accelerates,
The ship, sucked down the Rabbit Hole
Into a phantasmagoric
Wonderland of total darkness.
Intense gravity contorts my body,
My bulging eyes nearly pop.
I feel squeezed to death's edge.

With a high voltage jolt, I awaken –
Or at least seem to –
Uncertain whether I had just died
Or was rescued by an unseen force
Stronger than a black hole's death-grip.
Had I just relived Poe's story,
"The Pit and the Pendulum"? –

My nightclothes soaked,
My heart racing out of rhythm,
My mind a shimmying torso.

I do not recognize where I am,
Or remember where I had been –
Who is this who writes these words?
Time has disfigured me,
All light sucked out,
All life disappeared –

Only the insatiable
Black vortex remains.

Straight Party Line

My moment in the voting booth
Has at last arrived.
I stand, ballot and marker in my hands,
Relieved I have nothing more to ponder,
Nothing to decide,
No hard choices,
Everything was clear
From the outset of this campaign.

Our way
Or their way.
What's there to think about?
Our candidate will rescue us;
Their candidate will destroy us.
No ballot ever
Easier to complete –
To follow a strict party line.
A single box to fill in –
Turn it completely black.
I feed my ballot to
The electronic machine –

Then leave –
Not smug,
Just right.

Inside the Ice Storm

Inside a foreboding night sky
van Gogh or Munch might have painted,
freezing rain falls and falls,
seductively coats
large limbs and tiny branches
till ice sparkles on its prey.

No good can come of this,
as ice soon measures
a half-inch thick and makes
every tree and plant bow low.
Soon ice will break the back
of trees fresh-shorn of leaves;
and winter, oblivious to any calendar,
will settle in and take possession
of everything in sight.

World Renewal in Winter

Winter makes its way
Toward us
As the sun sinks
Lower and lower,
Stays away
Longer and longer,
Could descend so deep
As to disappear forever –

      Will our sun abandon us
      To eternal night?
      Will we perish
      With vanishing light?

Let us, then, exalt
In festive jubilation –
Bright candles, Menorahs,
Yule logs, wood fireplaces,
Strings of electric lights
Woven around indoor Christmas trees,
And outlining the roof outside –
Everywhere redemptive light.

With fire and revelry

We emulate the gods
As we banish darkness
From our midst.
Maybe the gods
Will remember our plight,
Sense our trembling behind the gaiety.

    Can we conjure the gods by our flames?
    Can we soften their hearts by prayer?

We hope they will
Restore to us
The gift of life,
Renew the dimming world
Once more –

Our sun returned,
Winter's dread defied,
A world reborn.

Unclaimed

I show up on your doorstep;
You decline even to greet me,
But only say, as your index finger
Points far away,
"You do not belong;
You are not from here;
You can never be
One of us."
I see in her eyes
and in her forearms,
tightly locked against her chest,
that she will never claim me
as related to her in any way.

Dejected, I turn to leave,
But say first to her,
Looking into her frozen face:
"I am the stranger
You once were –
And fear again to be.
You were unclaimed
And cannot recognize
Yourself once more in me."

Pronouncement

For how long have you told me
I do not belong?
Each time I wince at your pronouncement –
Until one day you colonized my soul,
Your voice overtook mine,
Now mine makes the cruel announcement.

Conversation with an Innkeeper

Driving on the road in southwest Oklahoma,
Early morning before daylight,
I was in the motel lobby,
Getting a donut and orange juice,
Making polite conversation
With the innkeeper, when he remarked:
"You look like home is far away from here."

I muddled through excuses to divert him
From his observation:
"I've worked and lived
Around here for twenty-five years,"
I countered – hoping he'd forget
What he'd noticed at first glance.

"I'm originally from Back East, around Pittsburgh,
But that was a long time ago," I protested
With more irrelevant detail, like a decoy
To a hunter who had cornered his prey.
I drank my juice and ate my donut.

We wished each other well
As I walked out the door.
We both knew he was right.

Neighborhood Convenience Store, USA, 2018

"Bottom Feeders,"

What an old friend
In the medical field
Calls them.

"They don't eat healthy."
"They don't live right."
"Most of them are obese,"
"A time bomb for bad disease."

Always *They, Them* –
Blacks, Hispanics, even many whites.

Called "neighborhood convenience stores"
To make them sound homey, part of "us,"
Strategically located for people
Who mostly have neither cars nor pickup trucks,
Nor nearby city buses;
Only legs and feet to walk miles;
If they are lucky, a few relatives in town who might
Sometimes give them rides;
At best old bicycles
With baskets on their handle bars.

They walk at all hours of day and night,
On sidewalks and in the streets,
Both arms hanging to their sides,
Carrying bulging paper and plastic bags
Filled with soda pop and beer,
Hot dogs and bologna,
Laundry soap and toilet paper,
Boxes from shelves and freezers
Stacked with foods steeped in
Sugars, fats, salt, and starches –
Little or no fresh fruit or vegetables
To be found here –
Maybe a few overly ripe,
overpriced, bananas from a basket
on the cash register counter.

This place offers what they can afford,
With little money or Food Stamps
Issued once a month.
Supermarkets lie
Far beyond their bodies' reach;
Most of these emporia of plenty
Have moved away,
Found it too expensive to stay.

Destitute folk on the margins
Trudge to run-down apartment buildings
And ramshackle shared rent-houses,
All within "walking distance"
Of the convenience store.

Neighborhood store patrons
Are mostly shadow people
Who come and go,
Hardly noticed by the traffic
That passes them by –

Faceless marks,
Good for profit,
And little more.

Unanswered Questions

Is impossible
ever possible?
Shall I renounce
hope that finding
will ever be matched
by being found?
I wander the earth
seeking you.
If I find you,
will your eyes
turn away from mine,
just when I thought
they had met?
If I find you,
will I be also found?

Winter Truth

Dunkel ist das Leben, ist der Tod.
—Gustav Mahler, *Das Lied von der Erde*

Spring – Promise of renewal
Blossoms and flowers' resplendent allure
Venus, Queen of the Night
Siren's call, enchanting love
Petals fall, trees scoured by wind
Green prevails

Summer – Promise of permanence
Mature, dense leaves
A thicket where lies can hide
Withstand summer's storms

Autumn – Promise of second spring
Flamboyant leaves' decoy
Brilliant colors from the first chill
Herald of endings – a brief affair
A lover's vow broken
absence and grief

Winter – Laughter at promises
Destiny mocks fatuous hope
Rebirth foreshadows its own corpse
But hides from knowing its own secret
Trees pared to the bone
Naked, bare, exposed

Winter at last speaks the truth
The others are pretenders

The Mirror

Mounted on a wall,
A large wood frame
Once held a mirror.
We stood and sat before it,
Recognized ourselves.
The inside frame
Now lined with jagged glass,
Is what's left of the mirror,
Scattered debris,
Shattered fragments,
On the floor below.
We still approach the empty frame
To seek ourselves,
Hoping the mirror
Will be restored.
But it never is—
Only sharp pieces
Of fallen glass.
Nothing and no one
Remain to be seen.
We have disappeared.

Winter's Hand

On the South Plains
a winter storm approaches
like a pink hand,
reaching north toward its prey –
the animated weather map,
a horror movie.
Fingers extend northward,
while the back of the hand
follows not far behind.
Waves of freezing rain
will gently wrap ice around
unsuspecting tree limbs
until they slowly sag;
some will snap and fall
from the weight.
Heavy branches will crash into roofs;
trees will topple and crumple cars and trucks.
The city mobilizes its entire fleet of ambulances
to rescue drivers and passengers
who will be crushed in collisions on slick roads.
The icy hand that reaches so far
will arrive at its destination
and take the city for its prize.

Two Poems in Japanese Forms

Stealth (tanka 5-7-5-7-7)

Fall arrives by stealth –
Just when no one is looking,
A few telltale leaves
Scrape along the dry sidewalk.
Soon, there is no turning back.

Untitled (senryu 5-7-5)
my cat naps with me
could we be the same species
where is my food bowl

What a Leaf Tells Me   for Peter Petschauer

after Gustav Mahler, *Des Knaben Wunderhorn.*

"to see a world in a grain of sand." William Blake.

Nested amid
Blackjack and post oak,
In the haven
Of my front porch,
Beneath an abundant
Late summer crop
Of ripe green leaves,
I am not alone.

With no forethought,
I pick up a leaf
Plucked from its branch
By the wind.

I hold the leaf by the stem,
Glide my fingertips over
The leaf's glossy surface,
Then upon its dull underside
Bulging with veins.

My leaf begins to speak,
Wishes to console me:
With me you are not alone –
I keep you company
Even when I am
Invisible to you.
After the harshest winter
Still I return once more.
I am but a wisp of time –
Though I rest in your hand,
You cannot yet fathom
What you cradle –
My long journey to you
Is always in your midst.
My ancestry dwells in me.

Come with me
To the place of my birth –
Of photosynthesis and chlorophyll,
A lineage that began
A thousand million years ago.

Between your index finger and thumb
You hold the history of the earth.
Time nests you
As much as all of us
Scrub oak leaves envelop you now.

Hold me, cherish me,
I delight in your touch –
That you noticed at all.
But think of me also
As your passageway
To retrace my long journey
To be here with you.
The pilgrimage through time
We have just taken –
Is now yours.

Any time you feel lost,
Just remember
You can find your way
Back to my shelter.
I thank my companion
For this astonishing visit,
Grateful to be comforted
By a leaf – wondering
Whether I had chosen
The leaf or the leaf
Had chosen me.

A Good Evening of Theater

Forget the lines –
The only thing
You need to know
About the play
Is whether to exit
Stage left
Or stage right.
Don't wait for applause—
The audience has already
Long since left.
They wanted to make sure
They never heard *you* speak.

Tiny Nail Holes   For Peter Petschauer

An incidental finding,
So easy to miss,
As a historian conducts
Research in Polish
Villages and towns
In the early 21st century.
Careful observation of place,
Sense of place and time,
Long interviews with people
About their history.

Out of the corner of his eyes,
He notices two tiny nail holes
On door frames of house after house,
Painted over, nearly disappeared.
Asked people about them:
Many claimed not to know,
Said the nail holes were there
When they moved in years ago.

Curious, the historian thought,
That these holes,
Always on the same spot on the outer
Door post,

And no one knew what they were,
Why they were there,
Who put them there, and for what.
That part of the past was fuzzy,
If not opaque, to them –
They had never thought to ask.

As they told their stories
To the attentive historian,
A few people said in passing
They thought Jews
Once lived here,
but had no idea when,
or why they left.
The 1930s and 1940s were
For them a hole in time.
Only a few remembered
The sudden disappearance
Of Jews during those years,
To places not far away –
The roundups, the trains.
The people who knew,
Or acknowledged,
That Jews had lived there,
Said they were mystified:
The Jews just vanished,
Evaporated to no one knows where.

The mostly Polish Catholic
Owners of these fastidiously kept homes
had no idea what a *Mezuzah** was,
Or that the secret of the nail holes
Was that the *Mezuzoth* had been
Ripped out by Jews
When they were forced to leave
Their homes, and Poles became
Their "rightful" owners.

---

* A *Mezuzah* (plural, *Mezuzoth*) is a small, rolled up, piece of parchment that is contained in a decorative case and inscribed with specific Hebrew verses from *Deuteronomy* in the Hebrew *Torah*. The case is then affixed to the door frame of the house, usually with small nails. https://www.myjewishlearning.com/article/mezuzah/

The Tenth Jew*

I know the Hebrew words;
I know the old gestures;
I know some of the chants;
I know how to read;
I know how to pray.

But I don't know whether
I believe it anymore.
Not that I have firm doubts,
Not that I have good reasons
Science would approve of.
I have a place of ache
Where once blessed assurance dwelled.

---

* **Poet's Notes**: This poem is inspired by an event and amplified by imagination. Many years ago, I attended a Saturday evening service at my synagogue. It was the weekly service in which we bid farewell to the Sabbath until her return the following Friday evening. The service was also a transition from the sacred day of rest and prayer to the ordinary six days of work.

One Saturday night, I quietly entered the small sanctuary and was welcomed as a hero. It was not that I was new. I had been coming weekly for a long time, but people expressed deep gratitude that I had come that night. I felt gratitude in turn for the gracious welcome but also was somewhat puzzled. What was all the fuss about, I wondered? As I took my seat, someone explained what should have been obvious to me—until I arrived, there had only been present nine adult Jews, and I was the tenth. That is, I had completed the necessary minimum of adult Jews required to conduct the full service. I will never forget that night.

I don't know why I go
To *Schul* any more,
Unless it's to be sure
There is a tenth adult Jew
So that others can pray
A complete service.
Maybe to be obligated
To them is reason enough
To continue to go.

Sakura, Cherry Blossoms

For Koji Takahashi: mono no aware ("the pathos of things")

Purest white,
Hint of pink.

Graceful blossoms,
Fragile blossoms,
You are on loan
From the wind.

Away to College

Away to college –
    we were so close,
    now you are gone....
    I instead of we,
    was instead of is—
    a new language
    for this new life.

The house reeks of ghosts;
remembering haunts the place,
absences I can almost touch.
Then there is all you left behind,
parts of stories I still can touch —
now you are gone from them.
Every place turns up a memory
like an ambush.

Wherever I turn, I lose you again.
I wander the Oklahoma prairie
the way Lord Byron's Manfred
wandered the Alps.
I search for you in farmsteads,
in wheat fields, in grain silos,
in sunsets, in storms,

125

on every horizon.
I encounter you
in the most unlikely places,
then you vanish.
I keep losing you to the wind.

Fly Fishing Lesson

In memory of Dr. Robert Young

A wheat farmer fly fishes
In his favorite pond –
The only vacation he knows –
Wades near the shore,
His fly line out fifty feet
Into the water, the deceptive fly
Floating, lazy on the surface –

A scene that could be
Lake Placid, mirror-glazed,
Still, serene, the farmer
Waits, unhurried in his reverie,

For an unsuspecting fish
To lunge at his
Hook-concealing fly.

In his zone of suspended time,
The farmer could not
Know of the drama
Unfolding beneath the surface

Of this tiny
Sea of Tranqulility.

Not far below,
An unusual fish hesitated
To leap at the apparent fly
That lay motionless
Above him.
He had studied
This eerie situation
Many times before,
As one after another fellow fish
Pounced upon the fly,
Only to disappear instantly
Straight out of the water,
A hook piercing its mouth,
Attached to some sort of string or line.
But then taken to where? He wondered.

He imagined his fate to be theirs
If he succumbed to his appetite
Instead of to his eyes.
Though he was hungry,
He would wait.
His would be a better fate
Than that of his fellow fishes.

For now, he would sit back
Observe, and ponder
This unusual sight.
If this fish could not discern
The hook behind the lure,
He would at least
Not take the bait.

The farmer, feet firmly planted
On the bottom of the pond,
Out-waited many fishes.
After a few hours,
His vacation over,
He left for a few weeks
To work his farm,
He always returned
With a full box of flies,
Ready to resume
His calming sport of deception.

Meanwhile, the canny fish
Continued to encircle
Each new fly he saw,
Inspected it, waited,
And only went at the fly
He knew was safe to eat –

The fish knew nothing
Of the farmer
And his brief
Respite from toil –

He only knew that
Sometimes it is good
For a fish to learn
When not to bite.

Too Painful to Notice

For how many decades
of lost spring have I
failed to notice your arrival?

Can yearning be so immense,
despair be so leaden,
that I cannot bear
to give myself over to

> the white sea of Bradford Pear blossoms,
> the unfurling of purple redbud,
> the jaunty heads of yellow jonquils,
> the fiery reds of plump azaleas,
> the fluffy white seeds of cottonwood?

What is spring
to eternal winter?
Winter's desolation
lasts not a season.

Perpetual winter
is a curse.
Who will dispel it
and let you in?

Your Frown

You are dead – how hard it still is to say –
But your frown, your scorn,
Are still alive in me.
I see your angry face
As if you were still
Standing before me.
Though we buried you,
I cannot keep you away –
Nor would I wish to,
For you were gentle, too,
And I would keep you
For a comfort,
But your grimace shows up
Like a ghost, unbidden,
Condemning me to a
Life sentence of your fury.
I wish I could repel you,
But I cannot. I sometimes think
That my dying would end
Your vicious gaze,

But you, no doubt,
Would follow me to hell –
Though, come to think of it,
I can think of no worse
Or more permanent hell
Than your disapproving face
In this life.

Signs of Spring

Spring is a sign
Winter has passed through
And will do so again –
But is a long time until then.

New green sprouts everywhere
Infant, toddler, juvenile –
Gentle pastel hues before
Leaf and grass harden
Into summer's deep green.

Spring is no time for memory,
Only for promise,
For renewing hopes
No winter could conceive.

In giddy spring,
Who thinks of somber fall?

Shelf Life

For Seth Allcorn

Grocers talk of the shelf life
Of food in cans, jars, bottles, boxes....
I inspect plastic-wrapped
Cheese and bread for the first sign
Of putrid green mold.
Fresh meats and frozen fruits
All have labels on their wrap
That read Best Used by This Date –
When wholesome food turns to rot.
All my medicines
Come in bottles
Somewhere stamped
With an expiration date,
The moment white magic
Decays into black magic.
How much battery-life
Remains in these once-new
Alkaline AA cells I discover
Deep in my kitchen drawer
Years after I had placed them
There just in case
My own ran out of juice?

I dwell on cliff's edge
In this sputtering body,
Worn down by how it lived.
Scars on the surface
Hint at sordid stories beneath
That had been cut out
Or repaired just in time.
Eventually I begin to wonder
How much shelf life I have left –
What would the grocer say?

Existence

I exist in your eyes
until they drop me
and I am no more.

A Dot's Journey

First a thought,
Then a dot
With a circle
Faintly in mind.

The slightest line
Emerges from the dot,
Hesitates, its pseudopod
Ventures a tiny step,
Stops, extends but a hint more,

Begins to shape
Into a curve that
Turns slightly inward,
Halts once more before advancing –

Recognizes where
It is headed only
Upon arrival, followed
By the next amoebic
Dare of advance and curve –
Direction revealed
Only retrospectively –

Until the dot
Meets and reunites
With itself,
Quest and destiny
A circle, the first thought
At last complete.

Siege by Ice

Freezing rain fell throughout the night,
Enveloped trees and power lines
The way venomous snakes coil themselves,
Ready to strike their unsuspecting prey.

Ice-laden branches,
No longer able to bear their weight,
Snapped, fell upon roofs of homes.
Whole trees, uprooted,
Smashed everything in their path.

Electric transformers exploded.
Entire neighborhoods went dark.
Inside our home,
We prepared ourselves
With candles and flashlights,
But could not sleep, waited instead
For the next alarming snap.

Daybreak and sunlight offered no relief.
Eyes confirmed what ears had guessed
During the ice storm's rampage –

Our driveway had become
An impenetrable thicket
Of ice-laden tree limbs
That refracted light with blinding glare.

A night of freezing rain
Had become a night of terror –
Were we forever sealed
Into our own home,
Our refuge now a tomb?

Too Much

In the long shadow
the Dust Bowl casts,
we dare not think,
let alone say,
"...just too much rain."
We celebrate green.
Dire fear of drought
makes us bear flooding,
clean up the mess, rebuild,
and go on down the road.
This time, we say hesitantly,
"It's too much,
too much rain,
too much ruin,
too much death."
This time — as we hold our breath —
we pray for the rains to stop —
at least for a little while.

Love Song to the Rocks of Ghost Ranch, NM

In the high desert
Of northern New Mexico,
On the floor of
A tropical inland sea
Dinosaurs once called home,
Red sandstone and shiny rose quartz,
Mesas and canyons,
Buttes and spires,
Speak in the tongue
Of two hundred million years.

Monuments to time tower here –
Fathomless sky crowns
The kingdom of stone below.

What tough skin, these old rocks,
Faces weathered and pockmarked.
I touch you,
You touch me back
With your craggy, coarse texture.
Your ruddy glow in a low sun
Unmasks your tender countenance;

143

Mute rock cannot conceal
Your comforting presence.

How to wrap my arms around
The "Valley of the Shining Stone"?*
My eyes do no better
Than my outstretched arms,
To embrace a space
Not even mind can hold –
You are beyond compass.

* *"el Valle de la Piedra Lumbre"* (Spanish), in the Chama River Basin

Cliffhanger

To the memory of Dmitri Shostakovich

A nominally successful
Murder mystery writer
Of short stories and an occasional novel,
Read from his work at public literary events,
Signed copies of his novels here and there.
During interviews at public libraries,
And on radio talk shows,
He kept coming back to the term,
"Cliffhanger" to describe his style
Of writing plots –
He liked to keep people "on the edge,"
He said, in suspense,
And in a sense of imminent danger
To the very last moment,
So near the cliff's edge,
They could easily
Lose their balance and slip off –
But at the last moment
Were miraculously rescued
By an unexpected turn in
the story's plot.

A curious TV interviewer
Recently pointed out to him

That he frequently spoke of his
Murder mystery writing style
In images of *cliffs* and *cliffhangers*
And *precipitous edges.*
He acknowledged these
Were also conventional terms,
But wondered whether they
Had any special significance for *him.*
Had his guest ever given thought
To this recurrent choice of words?
No – the writer said, first slowly, then puzzled,
At least not until this moment
When he had been asked.

Silence.
Suddenly, he was ambushed
By an imminent sense of danger,
Then a vague memory of
His grandmother's account of
Long ago when the Nazi army
Invaded Kiev, Ukraine, in 1941.
Soldiers murdered tens of thousands
of Jews systematically,
Lined them up in wave after wave
At the edge of a steep cliff,
Then machine-gunned them down,
Their dead or half-dead bodies

Falling backward into a deep ravine –
An assembly line,
Its only product, death.

Both writer and interviewer,
Stunned by the story
They had just stumbled upon,
Sat choked up and silent.
The camera crew sensed
This to be a profound moment,
And continued taping the two men
who remained speechless in their grief.
Eventually, they spoke about
This miracle of realization
That had just occurred,
And concluded the interview.
Uncut, it would
Later be shown on TV.

The place of the massacre
Is called Babi Yar,
A huge and deep ravine outside Kiev.
That is where the first
Cliffhanger had taken place,
And where there was no return
From edge of the cliff.

Good Company

Ambling toward me from the pond,
the ducks approach with hope,
maybe even longing,
no doubt with bread in mind.
They find me empty-handed, though.
For ducks' reasons I cannot fathom,
they gather around me, crouch,
and stay. I had never
fancied myself
a substitute for bread.
Still, the thought gives me comfort.
We, the ducks and I,
keep each other good company.

Exile *in situ*, A Protest Soliloquy

Many voices have
Given me these words;
I pass them on
To you —

What we have long called home,
you call wilderness,
to do with as you please.
You defiled our ancestral land.
You profaned our sacred trails.
You poisoned our earth
and our streams with your atomic waste.
You made us homeless in our own home.
You uprooted us in space and time.
You sowed chaos in the universe.

How do we repair what you have broken?
Can our ceremonials and offerings
bind the earth together once again?
Is renewal possible?
What holy power can
fend you off?
Is there a medicine bundle
that can heal us?

Signs

On a four-lane road in-town
I drive west toward home.
I approach a road sign
On the right:
"Work Area Ahead."
Soon another instruction:
"Right lane closed ahead."
Shortly thereafter, as
All traffic slows down,
"Merge to the left, single lane."
Then, "Two lane traffic ahead."

I do not drive for long
In single file
Before a huge construction site
Emerges on the right.

Only slightly further down the road,
Another road warning appears:
"Road closed ahead
To all traffic."
I wonder whether the next
Sign will tell us
Where to turn off

Onto a detour
That will return us
To our original path.
Instead, a series of messages,
"Do not go here,
Do not go there."
Side street access
Also blocked everywhere,
Each with its own sign.
I look for detour notices
To appear. My body
Braces for danger.
I begin to worry, as if
Something ominous
Is occurring. Still,
The words on the signs read
Matter of fact," as though
Nothing here was unusual,
But like road construction
Sites everywhere.

As I inch along,
A bizarre sign appears:
"No detours available
At this time," shortly followed by
"We apologize
For any inconvenience."

Several houses further,
A final one reads,
"The Transportation Department
Is Working on a Solution."

I am stuck in an
Ever-lengthening
Line of cars and trucks.
What now?
Nowhere to go,
Nothing to do –

Maybe there never was.

On This Shore

In Memory of Simcha Stein, 1992–1998

We walk but for a time
On this shore.

It soothes our feet;
It swallows up
Our footprints.

It makes sandcastles
Of our empires
And of our dreams.

It washes our conceits
Far out to sea.

The shore keeps us company
Until it must go on.

Spring's Herald

After so rogue a winter,
Ambush of delight –

A solitary dandelion's
Long, narrow petals
Speak bright yellow
To the still-silent sod.

Herald and scourge,
Lower than amoebae
On the evolutionary
Ladder of taste,
This unwelcome weed proclaims,
"It is time to awaken!" –
The still-frozen world
Renewed by a pest.

Stealth

Fall arrives by stealth –
Just when no one is looking,
A few telltale leaves
Scrape along the dry sidewalk.
Soon, there is no turning back.

Under New Management

Oceanside Seafood and Steak
Under New Management
Closed
Brooks Real Estate

Mario's Italian Pasta and Pizza
Under New Management
Closed
Sunshine Real Estate

Fiesta Restaurant and Cantina
Under New Management
Closed
Boardwalk Real Estate

Roy's Homestyle Cooking
Under New Management
Closed
Roseridge Real Estate

What's wrong with this place?
If it's the old saw: "Location, location, location,"
Is the ground haunted –
By the first merchant

Who found quicksand here
Instead of fortune,
And placed a curse on
Any future shopkeeper
Who dared try to better him?

Does everyone who settles here
Share the doom
Of the Flying Dutchman?

Dictating Humor

After "Humor," by Yevgeny Yevtushenko; Symphony No. 13, Dimitri Shostakovich:

> "Tsars, Kings, Emperors,
> sovereigns of all the earth,
> have commanded many a parade,
> but they could not command humor."

Laughter erupted in the party congress,
Didn't matter who the speaker was –
Stalin, Hitler, Mussolini, Milosevic,
His joke was always funny, ribald humor,
Often its bite – maybe later, its gun –
Aimed at a dissident or defector
Or THEM, the enemy religion
Or nation or race.

Nothing was funnier than
Their leader's grotesque cartoon
Of the collective enemy, a menace
Who threatened them both from the inside
And from outside. Mockery made way
For rally, to defend, to protect, to attack,
Which drew vigorous, sustained applause.
Often the faithful even leapt to their feet,

Pumping the leader to tell even bolder jokes
And to draw with his words
Even more outlandish caricatures,
Followed by an even more urgent
Call to arms – with him
As their uncontestable leader.

Spontaneous laughter and applause
Were cued with precision – they knew
When to laugh, just as they knew
They were being watched by spies
Who would report if their response
To his humor was not enthusiastic enough.
Laughter on command – what a strange notion,
They briefly allowed themselves to wonder.
If you want to live, you'd better laugh –
Or get expelled or shot dead.

This humor was serious business.
As time went on, it was hard to tell
Who was a loyalist,
And who an opportunist.
Sometimes they didn't even know
Themselves whether they were
True believers. They did know
Their leader's humor had to be funny...

...Just like at work, as we sit dutybound
Around the corporate board room table
In a meeting run by our CEO,
With his strict, printed agenda –
Though he never lets a chance go by
To first crack a few jokes,
Wait for our obligatory approval,
Then warn us about our fate
With our competitors
And our shareholders,
Who we can never feed enough –
Just as our overdone laughter
And sustained applause
Can never sate our CEO's
Ravenous appetite for approval and power.

At last, meeting over, we walk in open air,
Visit over coffee or a drink,
Truthful humor can return to our
Lips and voices, and laughs
Feel like our own again –

Though we still look
Over our shoulders, to check
Whether someone might be following us,

Listening for forbidden
Thoughts that made their way
Into our words and laughter –

Vigilant and wary,
Humor is never safe.

The Dead Tree

... stands sentinel

in most yards,
in most fields,
monument to death
in the din of life.

Surrounded by change,
the dead tree is changeless –
save for a telltale
bolt of lightning

that severs an arm
or splits the trunk
down the middle.
Generations pass;

the dead tree stays.
It does not speak,
but it passes judgment
on the living
who dare not
cut it down.

Triptych

Incarcerated
    by words
Liberated
    by silence
Redeemed
    by touch

Syllogism

Your intimidating words
Continue to ring in my ears
Long after you have hurled them.
They felt like a beating,
And my soul still smarts.
Just because you say
You don't remember,
Doesn't mean that
It did not happen.

By Order of the President, Invasion of the US Capitol, 6 January 2021: An Allegory.

To protect his country
From enemies that lurked outside,
The commander-in-chief assembled
The largest convoy in US history:
Aircraft carriers, cruisers, destroyers, frigates,
Littoral combat ships, merchant vessels, patrol ships,
And submarines.

One day he secretly issued an order
To all submarine captains to torpedo
The entire surface fleet, beginning
With the smallest, culminating with aircraft carriers.
Every ship must be taken out.
Faithful unto death, the submarine crews
Fulfilled their mission.

When the US Congress heard of the plan,
It was so divided it could not
Stop him. Every surface ship sank.

Strange, at the time he assumed command,
He took an oath of office to defend the Constitution,
And with it, the entire fleet in this armada.

Yet, from his first day in office,
He appointed officers who would sabotage
The task of every unit, and fired
Anyone who disagreed with him.

His order of an assault on the US Capitol
On January 6th 2021 was only
The most recent and brazen
Act of submarine warfare.
Though his offensive that day was foiled,
He and his immense wolfpack
Were heartened to be
Even more daring the next time.

Taking Notice

I sat on my porch
in a fierce summer storm,
beneath the shelter
of wide eaves.
Vertical bullets of rain,
razor lightning bolts, explosive thunder,
all so familiar – every storm
I had known over a lifetime
converged on this moment.
Past was now, making now
all the worse.
Today's storm violently merged with
and melted into my father's rages,
his vicious arguments with my mother,
our pleading with him not to leave,
her father's contempt for him,
my mother's suicide attempts,
my heaving sobs until blood flowed
from my nose onto the pillow
when I fled to my bedroom –
and the abiding dread
of pogroms against Jews.
In the midst of the storm's fury,
sudden calm –

an opening in the sky,
intense light broke through.
My eyes glanced upward;
for an instant
treetops glowed
in evening sun –
as if the earth had turned
and changed its mood.
Not intending to look,
I took notice
of the gift given,
though so brief the spell.
In waves of storm,
sunburst was exceptional;
the welcome interlude
was all too brief before
more grief set in.
(So too at home
when I was young.)
Soon chaos again
engulfed me.
The sky turned black,
sharp skeletal fingers of lightning
clawed the growing night.
Storms overwhelmed hope once again,
swallowed what light
had so fleetingly burst through.

I withdrew further under the eaves
as relentless rain returned –
rehearsing a lifetime
in a single storm.

Blessings of the Torah Reading

Jacob attended Sabbath and holiday services regularly for the past fifty years but now, frail and unsteady, he found everything to be effortful. Sensing his life was close to its end, he asked the rabbi if could chant the Torah blessing one more time.

His request granted, he struggled to climb the carpeted steps from the sanctuary floor to the Bimah. Several congregants sprang to their feet, gently but firmly grabbed Jacob's shoulders and arms, then steadied him as he haltingly walked to the ornate wooden table cradling the opened Torah scroll.

Standing securely, he stretched out his arm and touched the Tzitzit of the prayer shawl at the place where the master reader would chant the sacred text after the blessing, then
kissed the end of the fringes.

Jacob's once resonant baritone voice was now barely audible. The
first words, *Borchu es haShem ha'Mvorach* scratched out from his
throat. The congregation responded with its own brief chant. Jacob stood motionless. He forgot the next words and the music

he knew by heart. The reader, the rabbi, and the
cantor encouraged him, softly prompted the next few words
with
their melody. Jacob brightened, sang into the microphone.
Then
stopped again – each word, each phrase, insuperable.

A few congregants joined the liturgical leaders, then a few
more, until a groundswell of faint voices spread throughout the
congregation. Their unison wrapped Jacob in a giant prayer
shawl, restored his memory. Then together, as a single voice,
they
completed the Torah blessing.

When the prayer ended, everyone stayed standing, but in
silence,
in wonder, and in awe, to bless G-d who had given them such a
precious gift.

Poet's Notes: I am deeply grateful for John C. Mannone's generous help with
transforming my original poem into a prose poem.

In the Neighborhood

"Good fences make good neighbors." Robert Frost

In the neighborhood,
Houses, garages, cars,
Post oak, scrub oak, blackjack,
Occupy both sides of a narrow road –
The same species of trees,
An extended family,
Related by roots and acorns,
And in autumn, high waves
Of fallen leaves.

Our human neighbors are friendly,
Ready to help in some mishap –
But nonetheless distinguish "my trees"
From "your trees" – we all
Know the distinction.
Still, we call ourselves
A neighborhood;
The road is passageway
To get around in our community.

Squirrels and birds say otherwise;
Squirrels scurry across the inconvenience
As if they owned the place –

These are all *our* trees,
What matter *your* road to us?"
Birds, equally oblivious
To our boundaries and streets,
Fly, land, nest, raise families
In whose ever yard they choose –
Though they, too, have
Their own rules of spacing.

I cast my lot
With birds and squirrels,
And with their trees,
Who visit across the fences
We build to separate
Our real estate from our neighbors'.
Whatever our next barrier,
They will outwit
Our every property line
And zoning law –
What we build They will defy,
So long as this earth
Shall live.

Gliding

For Dr. Lisa Marotta

Such a simple, ordinary,
Thoughtful, gift to us,
Our group who meets most Fridays –
A ballpoint pen to celebrate
The opening of your new office.

I am a writer –
Pens and pads of lined paper
Are my dwelling place.

Parkinsonian tremor,
Loss of muscle strength
In my hands, and inability
To make my thumb
And index finger work together,
Turn handwriting into a seismograph,
Each twitch of the pen
Recording a minor quake.

My penmanship was never
Graceful ice skating to the music
Of a Tchaikovsky ballet.
Still, I never imagined

I would require a decoder
To decipher this monstrosity
Left on the paper.

Then you gave us
Your commemorative pen.
If a ballpoint could be redemptive,
This one is.
So smooth is its motion –
Makes the most perilous
Ballet maneuvers look easy –
When it rests between
My index finger and thumb,
It practically writes itself.
Though still no elegance
To this scrawl, I can compose
Without effort and can mostly
Recognize what I have written.

Your pen, no token, and I –
We glide together
On the ice.

After Franz Schubert

Beauty, loneliness, starvation, death —
so thin a membrane
between tuneful lyricism
and its twin,
outbursts of terror and despair.
Alloyed with cheer and high spirits,
horror and dread.
The lovely miller's daughter will spoil;
winter journeys do not promise spring.

My love, shall I pluck you a flower,
then dig you a grave?
Mine will soon follow.
Simple joy on the meadow;
a volcano erupts from beneath,
spews ash high into the sky.
Quiet meadows do not last.

How much darkness
can this light dispel?
Song triumphs
only for the moment;
melody is miracle.

Beauty spoiled by death;
death spoiled by beauty.
Terror despite beauty;
beauty despite terror.
Courageous Franz, tell me:
How could you live your brief life
poised at the edge of a cliff?

Splashings

Dedicated to three generations of Michael

Forty years in the steel mill,
From laborer to machinist –

His father, a struggling farmer
In eastern Slovakia, could not make
A life for his young family with such
Rocky soil, brought them
To America in mid-1920's,
Settled along the Monongahela River
Flood plain, rich in steel mills, and jobs,
Got work as laborer in the mill
To escape the squalor
Of unyielding earth
And no future, only to be
Ridiculed as a lowly "mill hunky"
By fellow steelworkers, who traced
Their roots to northwestern Europe,
And did not know the difference
Between Slovaks and Hungarians.
Much of his work life orbited around
Sweltering blast furnaces
And basic oxygen plants,
Where molten steel was
Poured into ingot molds –

And a blessed paycheck.

His young son, later my friend for decades,
Took a job in the mill, joined families
Of three and four generations of steelworkers
Like his own – but had aspirations
Beyond a lifetime as a manual worker.
He went back to school to learn a trade,
Became a machinist, returned
To the steel mill, carried
His phone with him everywhere –
He had the run of the place –
Drove his cart throughout the mill
Called to repair blast furnaces,
Cranes, and railroad locomotives,
With ingenuity beyond belief,
Improvisation his alchemy
That few understood.

At heart he was an artist –
Long evident in the ingenuity
With which he fixed things in the mill –
Metal sculptor, painter on canvas with enamels
Of mill life and of tools of every kind,
Filled sketchbooks with charcoal drawings,
And filled thousands of pages of notebooks
With dreams and yearnings about

Nature, the Universe, God, love,
His Slovak land and people,
His life from childhood in a village between
The Tatra and Carpathian Mountains,
To his eight decades in the Steel Valley
Of western Pennsylvania.
He never thought aloud of himself
As chronicler and witness,
But through his art, he was;
Art was his door to freedom.

He built an extensive workshop
In the basement of his own
Young family's home, then
Later an adjoining additional
Space to work, write – and *store*.
Dozens, then hundreds of boxes
Of all sizes to house his collections,
Some for current projects, most
For the future. His wife and son
Lived with and watched his unbridled
Imagination, his endless projects,
Most unfinished at his death
In his nineties. He could not
keep up with his accumulations –
Nor could they.

In the mill, during the long spaces
Between calls and urgent repairs,
He sat and wrote and sketched
In his notebooks. Every place he drove
He would stop his cart, get out,
Keep a safe distance
From the hot metal,
Then pick up several
Shapeless metal *splashings*
Strewn all over the mill ground,
As molten steel was
Being poured into ingot molds
And transported by ladle cars.
Spashings were his
Prize and treasure –
Testimony to the searing heat,
Dirt, toil, imminent accident,
And death only a second away.

Steelmaking's precision was
The twin of chaos and disaster.
His splashings were the raw material
For transmuting ugliness and peril
Into beauty and form.
Imagination and welding tools
Were his paint brushes;
With them, he could turn

181

Random shapelessness
Into his own design. What had
Begun life as liquid metal on filthy ground
Could be shaped into art,
Suitable for display on a bookshelf
Or a table.

Late in life, he gave me
One of his sculptures and several
Of his raw, slowly rusting, splashings.
I keep them close in the room
Where I write – an assortment
Of nails holds the splashings
On walls. His sculpture reigns
On the low windowsill
In front of my favorite chair.

I knew that behind these gems
Lay his massive collection
Of boxes of raw splashings piled high
In his workshops and garage,
For a someday, perhaps, if . . . .
When he died, his son, now my cherished friend,
Gave away several *tons* of his father's
Accumulation of splashings.

Maybe splashings are metaphor
For much of his own life,
Though he never said so.
Cast about in time and space,
This machinist and artist and dreamer
Took into his mind and hands
The chaos life had given him,
Gave it shape and form,
And turned refuse into art.

Fulness of Fall

I linger in the woods
Long after the leaves
Have passed their peak.
I await sunset through bare limbs.

Summer was a fine dream,
And spring is for next year's sprigs.
It is time now
For the fullness of fall.

Ripe Leaves

"Ripeness is all." *King Lear*. William Shakespeare.

Tough lives, tougher hides,
Texture of perseverance –
Scrub oak leaves,
Mature by late spring,
Await a beating sun
In summer's drought.

    Broad, hand-shaped;
    Deep, glossy green on top,
    Fuzzy, pastel matte beneath;
    Its bulging veins distribute
    Precious nutrient brought
    From distant lands,
    Root to trunk to branches,
    Smaller and smaller,
    At last, to their destination,
    Leaves to store
    When the supply chain ceases
    From long spells without rain.

Backlit in evening sun,
Thousands of tiny, translucent,
Stained-glass windows
Stage a magic show
From the ends of their narrow twigs –
Gift of delight
In their hardscrabble life.

These rugged leaves
Know nothing of their fate –
If only for a summer,
Ripeness prevails.

Diminution in Autumn

The rhythm of seasons
Soothes me in its cycles –
Spring, summer, fall, winter,
Lost, but later found,
Leaving, then returning,
Blessed Assurance,
Promise unbroken,
In Nature's circle,
I am completed anew
For another year.

Autumn, though,
Sometimes is different –
Fall makes no vow for spring;
Yields only to winter,
As far into the future as it
Is allowed to see.
Maybe there is no Promised Land,
Nothing beyond a wall of ice.
Endings cannot assure beginnings,
When endings are all they know.

Maybe spring will not follow
This year. Even circles
Have exceptions.
A pungent scent rises
From decaying leaves,
Soggy from recent rain –
Maybe this is the best
Any fall can do.
Maybe full circle is
Wager and conceit,
Our geometry wrong;
Sometimes a tangent
Drifts so far from its circle,
The circle vanishes –
From sight, from thought.
Did the circle ever really exist?

How can autumn yearn
For a spring it can no longer imagine?
Sometimes a tangent,
Lost in space and time,
Cannot find its way home,
Or even remember home.
Only autumn and perishing
Remain of what
Was once a full year.

Among My Scrub Oak

leathery leaves
contorted branches

not much for majesty
not much for lumber

long roots for drought
long waits for rain

Oklahoma scrub oak
keep their secret
in carefully guarded rings

tell a story
of craggy defiance –
when most everything
around them dries up,
scrub oak still thrive

Two Bradford Pear Trees (*Pyrus calleryana*)

Two Bradford Pear trees
Have long stood watch
In the front yard
Of a wood frame farmhouse,
Surrounded now by city.
Today white blossoms burst
Their wintered crypt,
Proclaim spring's arrival.

I have had the same delight
As I walked by these trees –
Nearly always pausing –
For over thirty years.

In this hall of time's mirrors,
I can see far back,
Remember seeing farther back.
I gather all those years of blossoming
Into a comforting wreath.

In the front yard
Of a weathered farmhouse,
Two Bradford Pear trees
Renew me once again.

The Marx Brothers Come Home

"Let me help you out. Which way did you come in?"; "You should go far – and I hope
soon." Ruth Stein (the poet's mother, circa 1950's)

No one could have
Planned it to come out this way –
My son, Zev, now 28,
Incarnates the Marx Brothers.
It proclaims itself everywhere:
In his gestures; in phrases

From all their films, in his quick wit
From Groucho's television
Quiz show, "You Bet Your Life."
Twenty or so years ago I bought him
A boxed set of Marx Brothers movies –
He soon memorized them,
Enacted scenes from them.

"Who are you going to believe, me or your own eyes?"
(Chico Marx, *Duck Soup*)

He does not quote or imitate;
Their words flow from his mouth
And gestures from his body
As though they were his own –

By now they are. His timing
Is impeccable. Caricaturist
And social critic, he is
Unassailable because he looks
So irreproachably ridiculous.

"If any form of pleasure is exhibited, report to me and it
will be prohibited." (Groucho Marx, *Duck Soup*)

Take Groucho's deep, stooped posture,
His body bent nearly 90 degrees at his waist,
His exaggerated long steps,
One hand in the small of his back.
When I watch Zev's identical stride,
For a second, I do not know
Who I am observing.

"Time flies like an arrow, but fruit flies like a banana."
(Groucho Marx)

Since Zev's childhood, the Marx Brothers'
Zany movements and pithy quips
Have long taken up full time residence
In our household – he caught my every move,
Then took them in for himself,
Still does, first in his visits from college,
Later in his meals at home

On holidays from work,
And now in his role as my caregiver,
When in my seventies, I became beset
With illnesses and disabilities.
His humor lightens their weight.

"Why don't you bore a hole in yourself and let the sap run
out?" (Groucho Marx, *Horse Feathers*)

So, who are the Marx Brothers?
Actors, characters, dream team –
Audacious language and bridge
Between father and son,
Their humor, now
Life itself.

Mirror Image[*]

Just before sunrise,
I await at my window
Scrub oak trees
Across the street
To the west
To be brushed golden
By sun's first rays –
To greet the day,
To feel the earth
Turn on its axis
Beneath my feet.

Just before sunset,
I walk westward
Up my driveway
To the street,
Turn toward scrub oak
To the east –
Await the final
Alchemy of low sun
And atmosphere
To brush craggy bark

---

* previously published in *AWEN* (Issue 112, May 2021; Atlantean Publishing, Essex, UK).

With nightfall's gold –
To bid farewell
To day, if I must –

To sleep and hope
To awaken once again
Before the sun,
To observe with wonder
Its brief deposits of gold
On scrub oak,
Now once again
To the west.

Sometimes I wonder
If I am called upon
To bear witness
To this ancient
Rhythm of
Arrival, departure,
And return
Of fleeting wisps
Of gold on lowly,
Coarse-furrowed,
Scrub oak.

Natural Disasters

Acts of G-d, Natural Disasters,
Names we give to devastation
We contend is out of human hands –
Hurricanes (typhoons), tornadoes,
Earthquakes, floods –
The culprit: Father G-d and Mother Nature.

Rising oceans, warmer seas,
Melting polar ice, methane release
From thawing permafrost –
All created in part by
Burning fossil fuels at such a heat
That we require even more of it
To sustain our expansive ways –
The culprit: ourselves,
No gratitude, no remorse,
Only more mining and
Fracking and drilling.

How unnatural, these natural disasters?
How G-d's acts are so much like our own?
The earth remembers –

Our myths and words
May kill us all.
We are the fathers and mothers
We defy.

First Snow of Winter

New Year's Eve, I went to bed early,
The hard-caked earth, barren and dry.
I awoke to delight, six inches of snow,
Treacherous wonderland, but wonderland still.
Sky Painter had done his job well,
A thick canvas of white
Left little room for darkness –
Mostly south side of tree trunks,
And underside of branches.
The gale that blew in the snow
Had passed eastward hours ago –
Now, only stillness and brilliance
From an unimpeded sun.

Seventy-five years of this same moment
In all the places life and work took me,
Each first snow, a new canvas,
A fresh painting, not a print;
Recurrence, an illusion –

Though our earth had completely
Encircled the sun, and winter
Arrived right on time.

I do not know how routine becomes amazement,
How old once again becomes new.
Am I the child who long ago
Encountered this scene for the first time,
And now each year's first snow
Revisits this forgotten enchantment
In new delight?
When now becomes then
And back to now once again?
I end with amazement just as I began –
Unable to surrender wonder to cliché,
When each year's first snow
Is like none before.

Where Time is Place, Ghost Ranch, Northern New Mexico

"Zum Raum wird hier die Zeit." ("Here time becomes space.") Richard Wagner, *Parsifal*

This place once grew giants —
Their anatomy,
Layer upon layer of mostly
Mudstone and red sandstone.
Giants have ruled the eastern
Colorado Plateau
For over 200 million years.
They all have names:
Mesas and plateaus, hoodoos and spires,
Gorges and canyons;
These ancient titans
Define the place.

The voice of place is
The voice of time.
Buildup and breakdown,
Sedimentation and erosion.
Time deposits sandstone cliffs,
Then time destroys them.
Time creates giants;

Time flattens giants.
Even giants' days are numbered.

As place becomes another place,
Invincible giants dissolve.
Ages before high desert,
These badlands were tropical
Inland sea and swamp:
Ferns and dinosaurs ruled.

People from everywhere
Make pilgrimages here to witness
Their dreams reach
Far into the sky –
Longing for permanence,
Seduced by magnitude,
We dream in monumental stone.
But maybe we already know
What we wish not to know:
Even giants are transient visitors.

The lesson of place is time.
Solid rock flows. Here is where,
But where is always when.
Without time, there is no place.
Place is noun; time is verb.
Time prevails.

Still... in the valley of fleeting giants,
Grandeur is no delusion.
To dwell among these giants –
No matter how temporary
They are in geologic time --
Is more real than anything
Imagination could make up.

Dialogue

Patient to therapist:
"I am so full of hate."
Therapist to patient:
"Whose hate are you filled with?"
Patient to therapist:
"Is that why I am hearing voices?"
Therapist to patient:
"Among all these voices,
Do you recognize *yours*?"
The patient erupted
In uncontrollable sobs.
The therapist waited,
Offered the company
Of silence as the patient wept.
Then, therapist to patient:
"I will help you get your voice back."
Patient to therapist:
"So *that's* what this is –
Voice lessons."
Then, for the longest time,
They spoke no words
Between them, but shared
The voice of silence
In their midst.

Ours

The earth is not ours.
Ours is to hunt and gather,
sow and harvest,
partake of and protect
this fragile place
that is our home.
Ours is to give thanks –
even if we do not know
for certain to whom.
Ours is to know that
we live in great debt
to the perfectly distanced orbit
of our pearl of the heavens.

Acknowledgments

Weston La Barre, the eminent psychoanalytic anthropologist and consummate writer, mentor, and dear friend, taught me how to listen to words, phrases, sentences, and always search for *le mot juste*. Aided by what he called his "silken lash," he helped me to become a better writer.

Seth Allcorn, my friend and co-author since the early 1990's, has encouraged my writing poetry – organizational and all else – and has helped me to have the elusive sense of being alive that I hope comes alive in my poetry. In the last several years, we have co-created some thirty poems, now assembled in a book, *Whiteboardings*, published in 2023.

Over my life as a poet, I have been blessed to have and to have had many editors and mentors who have been as patient and encouraging with me as they have been rigorous: to name but a few, Phil Floyd, Linda Cope, Maxine Austin, Vivian Stewart, Madelyn Eastlund, Joseph Epstein, Julie Damerell, Margaret Toohey, Johanna Shapiro, John Frey, M.D., Paul Gross, M.D., Jo Marie Reilly, M.D., Warren Holleman, Leah Maines, Steven Gordon, M.D., Irene Willis, John C. Mannone, Dustin Pickering, Michael Broder, and D. J. Tyrer.

Most recently, Tamar Schwartz, Assistant to the Editor, of International Psychoanalytic Books, has patiently, meticulously, and enthusiastically guided me through the submission and editorial process. Likewise, Larry Schwartz, Production Manager of IPBooks, has helped me navigate their organizational complexity.

Kathy Kovacic, the book's cover artist who, based on a long initial letter from me, from our subsequent correspondence, from reading the poems, and from her resonance with book's theme, designed the cover art that blew me away with its Rightness. In a single image, she condensed and evoked the atmosphere and theme of *the entire book*! You have my awe as well as my gratitude.

I owe to IPBooks Director, Publisher, and Editor-in-Chief Arnold Richards, M.D., my gratitude for his original invitation of my submission of a poetry book proposal to IPBooks, which, among its thematic areas, publishes psychodynamically-informed books of poetry. I appreciate his generosity.

Permissions to Reprint Poems, and Unpublished Poems

miller's pond poetry magazine: The journal is defunct/no longer has website. I offer my deep gratitude to its long-time editor and friend, Julie Damerell.

What Is a Door? *miller's pond poetry magazine.* Volume 19, Issue 1, Winter 2016. http://www.millerspondpoetry.com/index.php/issues/index.php?page=vol19web1#Howard F. Stein Accessed 6 January 2016

"Street Light in Winter," "Distance." *miller's pond poetry magazine.* vol 22, web 2. Spring 2019. http://www.millerspondpoetry.com/index.php/issues/index.php?page=vol22web2#Howard F. Stein 3 May 2019. Accessed 3 May 2019.

"Streetlight in Winter," *miller's pond poetry magazine* . vol 22, web 2. Spring 2019. http://www.millerspondpoetry.com/index.php/issues/index.php?page=vol22web2#Howard F. Stein 3 May 2019. Accessed 3 May 2019.

"Gliding, "*miller's pond poetry magazine.* Vol. 23, web #2. Spring 2020.
http://www.millerspondpoetry.com/index. php?page=vol23web2#Howard F. Stein 29 April 2020. Accessed 29 April 2020.

"Mind Tricks, "Be Mindful." *miller's pond poetry magazine.* miller's pond. Winter 2020. Vol23Web1.
http://www.millerspondpoetry.com/index.php/current-issue/vol22web3#Howard F. Stein. Accessed August 10, 2020.

"Whitman's Miracles, Further Evidence," *miller's pond poetry magazine. miller's pond poetry magazine.* Fall 2020. Vol23 web3. www.millerspondpoetry.com/ Accessed November 1, 2020.

"What a Leaf Tells Me," *miller's pond poetry magazine.* WINTER 2021. Vol 24 Web 1. *miller's pond.* winter 2021 (millerspondpoetry.com) Accessed January 6, 2021.

"Mirror Image," *miller's pond poetry magazine.* Spring 2021. Vol. 24, Web 2. miller's pond spring 2021 (millerspondpoetry. com)
www.millerspondpoetry.com/index. php?page=vol24web2#Howard%20F.%20 Stein Accessed June 1, 2021.

Songs of Eretz Poetry Review: permission to reprint not needed. I acknowledge, with gratitude, the *Poetry Review* and its editor, Steven Gordon, M.D., for publishing each poem.

"Old Pickup," *Songs of Eretz Poetry Review*. September 26, 2018. http://www.songsoferetz.com/ 26 September 2018. Accessed 26 September 2018.

"Too Painful to Notice." *Songs of Eretz Poetry Review*. Tuesday, September 18, 2018. http://www.songsoferetz.com/. September 28, 2018. Accessed 19 September 2018.

"Your Frown," *Songs of Eretz Poetry Review*. September 21, 2018. http://www.songsoferetz.com/ 21 September 2018. Accessed 21 September 2018.

"Away to College," *Songs of Eretz Poetry Review*. September 6, 2018. http://www.songsoferetz.com/ 6 September 2018. Accessed 6 September 2018.

"Good Company," *Songs of Eretz Poetry Review*. 26 July 2018. Accessed 26 July 2018. http://www.songsoferetz.com/

"Coalescences," *Songs of Eretz Poetry Review*. Summer 2018. http://www.songsoferetz.com/ 19 July 2018. Accessed 20 July 2018.

"The Tenth Jew," *Songs of Eretz Poetry Review*. 26 June 2018. Accessed 28 June 2018. http://www.songsoferetz.com/

"Sakura, Cherry Blossoms, "Existence," *Songs of Eretz Poetry Review*. 10 May 2018. Accessed 10 May 2018. http://www.songsoferetz.com/

"The Dead Tree," *Songs of Eretz Poetry Review*. 24 May 2018. Accessed 24 May 2018. http://www.songsoferetz.com/

"For Now," *Songs of Eretz Poetry Review*. 1 February 2018.
Accessed 1 February 2018. http://www.songsoferetz.com/

"World Renewal in Winter." *Songs of Eretz Poetry Review*.
DECEMBER 2019 "WINTER HOLIDAY" ISSUE. December
15, 2019.

http://www.songsoferetz.com/ 15 December 2019. Accessed
15 December 2019.

"Landscape and Dreamscape," *Songs of Eretz Poetry Review*.
Monday, September 2, 2019.

http://www.songsoferetz.com/ SEPTEMBER 2019, "PROSE
POEM" ISSUE. 2 September 2019. Accessed 2 September
2019.

"Siege by Ice," *Songs of Eretz Poetry Review*. Saturday, October
26, 2019. Accessed 26 October 2019.

http://www.songsoferetz.com/
October 2019, "HALLOWE'EN/HORROR" ISSUE .

"Stealth," *Songs of Eretz Poetry Review*. May 15, 2019.
http://www.songsoferetz.com/2019/05/ 15 May 2019.
Accessed 15 May 2019.

"Stealth," "My Cat Sleeps with Me," *Songs of Eretz Poetry
Review*.

http://www.songsoferetz.com/2019/05/mayjune-2019-
japanese-form-issue.html 15 May 2019. Accessed 15 May
2019.

"Into the Vortex." *Songs of Eretz Poetry Review*. June/July
2019. http://www.songsoferetz.com/ published June 16,
2019. Accessed 16 June 2019.

"Two Poems in Japanese Forms." *Songs of Eretz Poetry Review.* Wednesday, May 15, 2019. MAY/JUNE 2019 "JAPANESE FORM" ISSUE. http://www.songsoferetz.com/2019/05/ Accessed 15 May 2019.

"Winter Truth," *Songs of Eretz Poetry Review.* JANUARY/ FEBRUARY 2019 "WINTER" ISSUE. Tuesday, January 15, 2019. Accessed, January 15, 2019. http://www.songsoferetz.com/

"Signs of Spring," "Two Bradford Pear trees (pyrus calleryana)." *Songs of Eretz Poetry Review.* Saturday, December 19, 2020. Accessed July 14, 2021. WINTER 2020 "SPRING" ISSUE. www.songsoferetz.com

" Love Song to the Rocks of Ghost Ranch, NM." *Songs of Eretz Poetry Review* Sunday, June 14, 2020 http://www.songsoferetz.com/ . Accessed June 14, 2020. SUMMER 2020 "LOVE" ISSUE.

"Linguistics Lesson, or, Making a List and Checking It Twice." *Songs of Eretz Poetry Review.* Monday, September 14, 2020. FALL 2020 "POLITICS" ISSUE. http://www.songsoferetz.com/. Accessed 14 September 2020.
Monday, September 14, 2020. FALL 2020 "POLITICS" ISSUE
http://www.songsoferetz.com/ Accessed 14 September 2020.

"Love's Decorum," "Love Song to the Rocks of Ghost Ranch, NM," *Songs of Eretz Poetry Review.* Summer 2020, "Love"

Theme Issue. June 14, 2020. http://www.songsoferetz.com/ Accessed June 14, 2020.

"Fly Fishing Lesson," "Keeping Time." *Songs of Eretz Poetry Review.* MARCH 2020, "FANTASY & FAIRYTALE" ISSUE. March 14, 2020. Accessed March 14, 2020. http://www. songsoferetz.com/

"Keeping Time," *Songs of Eretz Poetry Review.* March 2020 issue. published Saturday, March 14, 2020. http://www.songsoferetz.com/ Accessed March 14, 2020.

"Riot of Roses," *Songs of Eretz Poetry Review.* Fall 2021. Accessed October 17, 2021. www.SongsOfEretz.com

"Blessings of the Torah Reading," *Songs of Eretz Poetry Review.* Fall 2021. Accessed October 17, 2021. www.SongsOfEretz.com.

"The Old Recliner," *Songs of Eretz Poetry Review.* Winter 2021/2022. January 11, 2022. www.SongsOfEretz.com. Accessed January 11, 2022.

"Dictating Humor," *Songs of Eretz Poetry Review.* Spring 2022. "Humor Issue." Published Friday, April 1, 2022. www.SongsOfEretz.com. Accessed April 1, 2022.

Harbinger Asylum: I acknowledge with gratitude the permission given to me from Dustin Pickering, editor, to reprint each poem.

"Chaos Theory," *Harbinger Asylum.* Winter 2019. Houston, TX: Transcendent Zero Press. Pp. 27-28.

"Fullness of Fall," "Sinking In," "Humpty Dumpty's Needless Fall," *Harbinger Asylum*. Spring 2020. Houston, TX: Transcendent Zero Press. Pp. 60 ("Sinking In"), 60-61 ("Fullness of Fall"), 62 ("Humpty Dumpty's Needless Fall").

"Walking to the Polling Place, November 2020, US"; "Cliffhanger." *Harbinger Asylum*. Pp. 76–78 (Walking), p. 78 (Cliffhanger). Transcendent Zero Press.

"Tiny Nail Holes." *Harbinger Asylum*. Transcendent Zero Press. Spring 2021.
www.transcendentzeropress.org. pp. 64–65.

New York Parrot: I acknowledge with gratitude the permission given to me from Dustin Pickering, editor, to reprint each poem.

"Two Short Poems by Howard F. Stein," *New York Parrot*. "Difference, A Riddle for the Age of COVID-19," and "Drought," *NEW YORK PARROT*.
https://www.newyorkparrot.com/category/education/literacy/ Accessed 21 May 2021. Published 21 May 2021. Accessed 21 May 2021.
https://www.newyorkparrot.com/two-short-poems-by-howard-f-stein/ Published 21 May 2021. Accessed 21 May 2021.

"Ripe Leaves," *New York Parrot*. April 2, 2022.
https://www.newyorkparrot.com/ripe-leaves-by-howard-stein/ Accessed April 2, 2022.

"Exile in Situ: A Protest Soliloquy," *New York Parrot*. (on-line). November 7, 2020. Accessed 13 July 2021. Exile in situ: A Protest Soliloquy by Howard F. Stein — New York Parrot. https://newyorkparrot.com/exile-in-situ-a-protest-soliloquy-by-howard-stein/

AWEN (Atlantean Publishing): permission not required. I acknowledge with gratitude the journal and its editor, D.J. Tyrer, for publishing each poem.

"Scrub Oak Branches in Winter's Night," "Cliffhanger," *AWEN*. 108 (May 2020). No page numbers. Essex, UK. https://atlanteanpublishing.wordpress.com/

"Straight Party Line," *AWEN*. Issue 111. February 2021. https://atlanteanpublishing.wordpress.com/

"Mirror Image," "Not 'Either/Or,' but 'Both/And.'" *AWEN*. Issue 112, May 2021. Atlantean Publishing. Southend-on-Sea, Essex, United Kingdom. https://atlanteanpublishing.wordpress.com no page numbers.

"Splashings," *AWEN*. Issue 118. November 2022. Atlantean Publishing, Southend-on-Sea, Essex, United Kingdom, atlanteanpublishing@hotmail.com no page numbers.

"Sometimes It Is Just What It Is," *AWEN*. Issue 119. February 2023. Atlantean Publishing. Southend-on-Sea, Essex, United Kingdom. atlanteanpublishing@hotmail.com no page numbers.

DOVETALES: I am grateful Carmel Mawle, founding director, for her permission for me to reprint each poem.

"Condolences, Post Mortem," "Moments of Connection," *DoveTales: An International Journal of the Arts.* "Empathy in Art: Embracing the Other," Ft. Collins, CO: Writing for Peace. 2018. Pp.205-206.

"Pronouncement, "Dialogue." *DoveTales: Writing for Peace.* Ft. Collins, CO. *Writing For Peace. DoveTales, An International Journal of the Arts,* Issue I – August 2019. Patricia Jabbeh Wesley, Guest Editor: August 2019. https://writingforpeace.org/howard-stein/ Accessed 1 August 2019.

"Pronouncement." *Writing For Peace: Developing empathy and peaceful activism through creative writing. DoveTales, An International Journal of the Arts, Issue I – August 2019.* https://writingforpeace.org/howard-stein/ Accessed 1 August 2019

The Journal of Psychohistory: I acknowledge, with gratitude, the permission to reprint the poems below, given to me from David Lotto, editor; and Susan Hein, Managing Editor.

"Exile: A Montage of Voices," *The Journal of Psychohistory.* 46(1) Summer 2018: 70–71.

"The Second Flood," *The Journal of Psychohistory.* 47(3) Winter 2020: 232–233.

"Body Language," *The Journal of Psychohistory*. 47(4) Spring 2020: Pp. 329–330.

"Train Ride," *The Journal of Psychohistory*. 48(4) Spring 2021. p. 329.

"'Who's on First./?' Revisited." *The Journal of Psychohistory* 49 (1) Summer 2021. Pp. 79–80.

"Masks and Eyes." *The Journal of Psychohistory* 49 (4) Spring 2022. p.325.

"Signs." *The Journal of Psychohistory* 49 (4) Spring 2022. pp. 323–324.

"A Shirt's Tale." *The Journal of Psychohistory*. 50 (2) Fall 2022. Pp. 161–163.

Poetry Monday/Internationalpsychoanalysis.net I acknowledge with gratitude, the permission to reprint the poems below, given to me by Irene Willis, Poetry Editor; and Tamar Schwartz, Associate Editor.

"Syllogism," "Mindfulness," "Our Lives in Silos." https://internationalpsychoanalysis.net/poetry-monday-march-2-2020/#more-88225 POETRY MONDAY: March 2, 2020. March 2, 2020. Accessed March 2, 2020. internationalpsychoanalysis.net

The Literary Parrot: I acknowledge with gratitude the permission to reprint given to me by its editor, Dustin Pickering.

"In the Neighborhood." *The Literary Parrot*, series two. Dustin Pickering and Mutiu Olawuyi, Editors. Houston: Transcendent Zero Press, 2021. pp. 152–153.

"On this Shore." *The Literary Parrot*. Houston: Transcendent Zero Press, 2021. P. 244.

American Diversity Report: I acknowledge with gratitude the permission to reprint given to me by John Mannone, poetry editor.

"Native Wit." *American Diversity Report*. ADR Poetry. April 19, 2022. https://adrpoetry.com/spring2022/april2022/native-wit-by-howard-f-stein/_Accessed April 19, 2022.

"*Kelipoth* – Broken Vessels." *American Diversity Report*. ADR Poetry. December 12, 2021. Kelipoth – Broken Vessels by Howard F. Stein – ADR Poetry. 12-12-2021.html Kelipoth – Broken Vessels by Howard F. Stein – ADR Poetry. Accessed December 12, 2021

"Two Crossings," *American Diversity Report*. ADR Poetry. January 11, 2022. /Two Crossings by Howard F. Stein – ADR Poetry.html About the ADR – American Diversity Report Accessed January 11, 2022. https://americandiversityreport.com

"Native Wit," *American Diversity Report*. ADR Poetry. April 19, 2022. /Native Wit. Howard F. Stein – ADR Poetry. April

2022.html About the ADR - American Diversity Report Accessed April 19, 2022. https://americandiversityreport.com

What Rough Beast (Indolent Books): I acknowledge with gratitude the permission to reprint given to me by Michael Broder, editor.

"The Race," *What Rough Beast/ Indolent Books.* http://www.indolentbooks.com/category/online-projects/ what-rough-beast/ posted April 1, 2020. Accessed April 1, 2020.

"A Good Evening of Theater," *What Rough Beast/ Indolent Books.* https://www.indolentbooks.com/what-rough-beast-poem-for-September-26-2019/ 9/26/2019. Accessed 26 September 2019.

"The Mirror," *What Rough Beast. Indolent Books/ What Rough Beast.* Poem for July 10, 2019. published 10 July 2019. Accessed January 20, 2019. https://www.indolentbooks. com/what-rough-beast-poem-for-july-10-2018/

Other:

"Shelf Life," In: *The Healer's Grief: Stories and Poems of Professional Grief.* Melissa Fournier and Gina Pribaz, Eds. Iowa City, Iowa: College of Medicine, University of Iowa:

2020. p. 67. Permission not required after first publication; acknowledgment requested.

"Coronavirus (COVID-19) 2020, or the Natural History of Disease." *Clio's Psyche.* 26(3) Spring 2020. Pp. 321–322. Permission to reprint given to me by Paul Elovitz, editor.

"Unclaimed," In: *What They Bring: The Poetry of Migration and Immigration.* Irene Willis and Jim Haba, Eds. New York: International Psychoanalytic Books, 2020. p. 99. Permission given by Irene Willis.

"Four Haiku," "Spring's Herald," *Floyd County Moonshine.* 11(2) Fall 2019: Pp. 111 ("Four Haiku"), 148 ("Spring's Herald"). Permission given by Aaron Lee Moore, Editor.

"Neighborhood Convenience Store," *Ascent Aspirations Magazine. Friday's Poems* 14 September 2018. Accessed 14 September 2018. Permission to reprint given to me by its editor, David Fraser.

"Unanswered Questions." *vox poetica.* http://voxpoetica.com/unanswered-questions/_
2 September 2018. Accessed 2 September 2018. Journal defunct.

"Taking Notice." *vox poetica.* http://voxpoetica.com/taking-notice/ 2 October 2018. Accessed 2 October 2018. Journal defunct.

"Coffee Cup," *vox poetica.* http://voxpoetica.com/coffee-cup/ 28 January 2019. Accessed 28 January 2019. Journal defunct.

"Winter's Hand," *vox poetica*. http://voxpoetica.com/winters-hand/ 24 December 2018. Accessed 27 January 2019. Journal defunct.

"Natural Disasters," *Friday's Poems. Ascent Aspirations Magazine.* October 19, 2018. http://www.davidpfraser.ca/fridays-poems.html Accessed 19 October 2018. Permission to reprint given to me by its editor, David Fraser.

"Inside the Ice Storm," *Oklahoma Today.* January/February 2018: 33. Permission to reprint given to me by its editor, Nathan Gunter.

"Ours." *Oklahoma Today.* March/April 2022. p. 39. Permission to reprint given to me by its editor, Nathan Gunter.

"For Whom Do I Say *Kaddish?" For Poetry.* December 2008. http://www.forpoetry.com/decemberfebruary_2008.htm Accessed 5 October 2020. Permission to reprint given by me by its editor, Jacqueline Marcus.

"By Order of the President, Invasion of the U.S. Capitol, January 6, 2021: An Allegory," *Clio's Psyche.* 27(3) Spring 2021: p. 288. Permission to reprint given to me by its editor, Paul Elovitz.

"Under New Management." *Maverick Magazine 17.* Published 04/7/2012. Journal out of print.

"Conversation with an Innkeeper." Unpublished poem.

"Backlighting in Autumn," Unpublished poem.

About the Author

Howard F. Stein, PhD, is Professor Emeritus, Department of Family and Preventive Medicine, University of Oklahoma Health Sciences Center, Oklahoma City, OK USA. Howard is an applied, psychoanalytic, medical, and organizational anthropologist; a psychohistorian; an organizational consultant; and a poet. Poet Laureate, High Plains Society for Applied Anthropology, and Psychohistorical Poet Laureate, he has written, co-authored, and edited 35 books, ten of which are books or chapbooks of poetry. He has authored and co-authored several hundred papers, chapters, and poems.

His most recent poetry books are: *Whiteboardings: Creating Collaborative Poetry in a Third Space* (2023) (co-authored with Seth Allcorn); *Presence – Poems from Ghost Ranch* (NM) (2020); *Centre and Circumference* (2018); and *Light and Shadow* (2018, 2nd edition). In 2020 he co-authored with Seth Allcorn, *The Psychodynamics of Toxic Organizations: Applied Poems, Stories, and Analysis,* which includes about 80 of his organizational poems (Routledge). He can be reached at hfs.dad@gmail.com; Cell Phone: 405-226-2484.